MARVIN KOHL

The Morality of Killing

SANCTITY OF LIFE, ABORTION
AND EUTHANASIA

PETER OWEN

London

ISBN 0 7206 0182 7

PETER OWEN LIMITED
20 Holland Park Avenue London W11 3QU

First British Commonwealth edition 1974
© Marvin Kohl 1974

Printed in Great Britain by
Clarke Doble & Brendon Ltd
Burrington Way Plymouth Devon

To my mother

MOLLIE KOHL

What no human soul desires there is no need to prohibit; it is automatically excluded. The very emphasis of the commandment *Thou shalt not kill* makes it certain that we spring from an endless ancestry of murders, with whom the lust for killing was in the blood, as possibly it is to this day with ourselves.

Sigmund Freud, 'Thoughts on War and Death' (1915)

Aggression, far from being the diabolical, destructive principle that classical psychoanalysis makes it out to be, is really an essential part of the life-preserving organization of instincts. . . . That indeed is the Janus head of man: The only being capable of dedicating himself to the very highest moral and ethical values requires for this purpose a phylo-genetically adapted mechanism of behaviour whose animal properties bring with them the danger that he will kill his brother, convinced that he is doing so in the interests of these very same high values. *Ecce homo*!

Konrad Lorenz, *On Aggression*

Foreword

The reader of this book on the nature of justifiable killing, abortion and euthanasia is in for an object lesson in what we might call essentiality. Marvin Kohl's approach to his subject shows us plainly how forceful a succinct explication of ethical questions can be. Most readers will agree, I think, that his critical manners are always sturdy and candid but never pugnacious.

Too few analytic philosophers have tackled the questions he examines. We need more papers like these on 'The Argument from Innocence' and 'The Slippery Slope' displaying Professor Kohl's developed reasoning; we need too such emancipating seminal observations as his remark that the *quid-pro-quo* or classical *suum cuique* notion of justice reduces morality to 'a niggardly form of obligation'.

I am struck too by his examination of compassion, love and benevolence. He shows us that it is easier (not easy, he is careful to note) to determine compassion when people are suffering, than to determine what loving concern or benevolence requires, when fully comprehended. Yet surely the problem of making loving concern the guideline becomes more manageable if we make the absence of suffering the first-order test for the loving moral agent, rather like Bentham's absence of pain. However even here, in the spirit of Professor Kohl's characteristic allowances for other positions, it is probably true to say that finite human beings cannot escape all suffering and that it would undermine their creativity if they could.

He explores euthanasia and the moral questions at stake in any proposed human initiative in terminating a life process, directly by commission or indirectly by omission. From this logical and balanced discussion emerges a reinforcement of the argument for 'moral' or 'kind' killing, as an ethical category.

New works on this subject often have a treadmill or threadbare quality. Not this one.

JOSEPH FLETCHER
Professor of Medical Ethics
School of Medicine,
University of Virginia

Contents

Preface

The purpose of this book is threefold : first, to provide a more adequate formulation of the principles of sanctity-of-life and self-defence; second, to explicate fundamental issues and thereby help to resolve the abortion controversy; and third, to examine the seemingly incongruous notion of kindly killing and make the case for beneficent euthanasia.

It is natural to feel some hesitation in publishing a work that praises some varieties of killing. But I offer it in the hope that it will induce pacifists and those opposed to abortion or beneficent euthanasia to reflect once more on the foundations of their philosophical thinking. For like death, killing is sometimes kind, and far too often it is the only means by which the oppressed or injured can protect their rights.

Four of the nine chapters have previously been published : 'The Word "Mercy" and the Problem of Euthanasia' in *The American Rationalist*; 'Abortion and the Argument from Innocence' in *Inquiry*; 'The Sanctity of Life Principle' in *Humanistic Perspectives in Medical Ethics*, edited by Maurice Visscher; and 'Abortion and the Slippery Slope' in *Dissent*.

Each chapter was written and stands as an independent unit. This means that the reader need not follow the ordering of chapters, but may choose freely according to his or her own interests. It also means that there is some, and in one chapter perhaps too much, repetition.

The writing of this book has been greatly facilitated by several persons, and it is a pleasure to express my gratitude. I owe a large debt to Sidney Hook, who both as teacher and philosopher stands as an exemplar of excellence. I am especially grateful to him for his kindness and patience. I wish to thank J. O. Wisdom for awakening me from my logical positivist slumbers by providing a richer, far more exciting, picture of what philosophy ultimately is about. I also wish to thank Jerrold J. Katz for deepening my understanding of semantics and for his warm friendship.

I want to express my thanks to Stephen Nathanson, Douglas Shepard, and Michael Walzer, who gave me encouragement and the benefit of their criticisms on various portions of the manuscript; to Harold Bleich, Charles Goodrich, Martin and Diana Livingston, Martin and Ruby Vogelfanger, Michael and Judy Walzer for their concern and help; to Robert Hoffman, who as a colleague and friend contributed significantly to the clarification of many of my ideas; and to my children, Richard, Rhiana, Matthew, and Maura, who have added much beauty to my life. Finally, I wish to express my gratitude to my wife, Phylia, for her sense of excellence, zest for life, and loving devotion.

MARVIN KOHL

PART I

Problems of Justifiable Killing

No man can win freedom and peace unless he conquers his fear of death. No nation can preserve its freedom unless it is willing to risk destruction in its defence. To do otherwise is to break faith with those who died to keep it free.

Sidney Hook, 'A Counter Rejoinder (to Bertrand Russell)', *New Leader*, July 7, 1958

I

The Sanctity-of-Life Principle

In this chapter I wish, first, to analyse different versions of the sanctity-of-life principle and inquire what, if any, justification there is for believing that life is sacred; and second, to point out certain confusions, especially in regard to euthanasia, that appear to be connected with the erroneous notion that one ought never to kill an innocent human being.

The analysis which follows does not purport to be exhaustive. I thought it better to make a reasonable case against more viable positions than to spend time refuting weaker ones. Hence I shall have little to say about the killing of animals or the claim that one ought never to kill any human being – not because these problems are unimportant, but because I feel that others are more important.

It is often said that 'human life is sacred'. This sentence is thought to express a 'sanctity-of-life principle', or 'SLP' for short. That men actually talk this way, that they use the same speech or orthographic patterns, does not mean that they are all saying the same thing, or that the principle is simple. In fact, the opposite is the case. The SLP is open to, and is often given, different interpretations. It is chameleon-like, changing its colours according to the moral theory it rests upon. It is almost as if a family of related but differing principles were hidden under the rubric of the SLP in order to give the impression of moral consensus.

Consider the following sentence-types:

    (1) One ought never to kill an innocent human being

3

because in some religious or protoreligious sense life is
sacred;

(2) One ought never to kill an innocent human being
because such an action would be unjust;

(3) One ought never to kill an innocent human being
because such an action may (or must) lead to undesirable
consequences; and

(4) The sentence 'One ought never to kill an innocent
human being' expresses an ultimate moral principle.

Generally speaking, Roman Catholic writers[1] emphasize (1), and
use (2) and (3) as supporting arguments. Albert Schweitzer[2] and
Edward Shils[3] seem to use (1) and (3) as complementaries, and
Yale Kamisar[4] and others use (3) to argue against euthanasia
legislation. (4) is important because it contains the word 'ultimate',
the ambiguity of which leads to the muddling of different claims.

Religious and Protoreligious Interpretations

I shall begin with a brief evaluation of traditional theism, then

---

[1] See: Charles J. McFadden, *Medical Ethics* (Philadelphia: F. A. Davis,
1967); Edwin F. Healy, *Medical Ethics* (Chicago: Loyola University Press,
(1956); and Norman St John-Stevas, *The Right to Life* (London: Hodder &
Stoughton, 1963; New York: Holt, Rinehart and Winston, 1964). Daniel
Callahan, 'The Sanctity of Life' and 'Responses' in *The Religious Situation
1969*, ed. D. R. Cutler (Boston: Beacon Press, 1969) does not make any direct
religious appeal, but concludes that the ultimate justification for a normative
principle is that it coheres with 'our entire reading of the nature of things' and
that it 'makes sense in terms of our metaphysics' (p. 359). The interesting
question is, from what metaphysic has he deduced or established his version
of the SLP?
[2] Albert Schweitzer, *Out of My Life and Thought* (New York: Mentor
Books, 1953), especially the 'Epilogue'.
[3] Edward Shils, 'The Sanctity of Life', in *Life or Death: Ethics and
Options*, ed. E. Shils *et al* (Seattle: University of Washington Press, 1968),
pp. 2–38.
[4] Yale Kamisar, 'Euthanasia Legislation: Some Non-Religious Objections'
from *Euthanasia and the Right to Death*, ed. A. B. Downing (London:
Peter Owen, 1969; New York: Humanities Press, 1970), p. 85–133. [Where
two editions of a work are given the page references apply to the U.S.
edition only.]

consider Schweitzer's approach, and conclude with Edward Shils's notion of a protoreligious metaphysic.

According to the traditional theist, God is a personal all-powerful being, a sovereign who rules over his creation. Hence :

> Man is merely the custodian of life, not its Master. . . . It is man's duty to accept the decisions of God, not to pass judgments on them. If God has created and bestowed life upon man, it does not fall within the right of man to destroy it.[5]

> Man is not absolutely master of his own life and body. He has not *dominum* over it, but holds it in trust for God's purposes.[6]

The difficulty is that if we grant that an all-powerful God has absolute sovereignty over human life, then if He himself held human life to be sacred, i.e., if He really cared, He would interfere. At least, He would cure the sick; at most, He would prevent unjust illness and accident. If He does nothing, we can only conclude that either His sovereignty is limited (meaning perhaps that He wants us to act), or His power is limited, or He simply does not care.

In other words, if God is what the traditional theist says He is, why doesn't He interfere in cases of unjust illness and accident? On the other hand, if God is not what the theist says He is, and does not interfere with nature – i.e., if He does not 'play' God – then either He wants us to make decisions and to act, or He does not. If He does not, then He is a non-moral god – at least, so it would seem to me.

Although this argument may be countered, it is not so easily met. For instance, someone may suggest that the existence of a moral God does not entail the conclusion that has been drawn. He probably would remind us that God is just, distributing happiness among men according to their deserts, but that this

---

[5] Charles J. McFadden, op. cit., p. 227.
[6] Norman St John-Stevas, op. cit., p. 12.

distribution essentially occurs after death. Hence, from this point of view, God is moral, even though it does not always appear so. This counter-argument is a variation of an old but ingenious attempt to explain away the existence of evil. But this eschatological explanation will not do; at best it is mere conjecture, and at worst, theological illusion. Moreover, when we examine the concept of morality as it seems to show itself in the words of Jesus and other writers, we observe that benevolence, or love, and related behaviour (such as self-sacrifice) are deemed to be necessary conditions. This would seem to indicate that justice in its narrow sense is not a sufficient condition for morality. A just God need be just, but He need not be moral.

One of the merits of Albert Schweitzer's approach to this problem is that he does not presuppose or establish a basic antinomy between God and man. God, as conceived of by Schweitzer, reveals Himself in the world as the mysterious creative Force, but within man He reveals Himself as ethical Will. 'All living knowledge of God rests upon this foundation : that we experience Him in our lives as will-to-love.'[7]

This manœuvre helps to avoid the major pitfall in the traditional theistic position. Since God, for Schweitzer, is part of the life force as ethical Will, God 'plays' God when man acts ethically. For, if I understand Schweitzer correctly, God expresses His sovereignty through man, and shares it with man. When we care, when we are concerned, He is also expressing care and concern.

Since God is in the world, and since He is part of the life force as ethical Will, it is necessarily true that if God is sacred, then life is sacred. Notice the beauty of Schweitzer's argument. All the statements are linguistically true. The logic is impeccable. And most important, it provides the grounds for the credibility of the sanctity-of-life principle.

Unfortunately, however, the argument is factually vacuous. That is to say, the premises are true, but analytic. The sentence 'God is in the world' is true because 'being in the world' is part

---

[7] Albert Schweitzer, op. cit., p. 184.

of what is meant by the word 'God'. 'God is part of the life force as ethical Will' is true because 'being part of the life force as ethical Will' is part of what Schweitzer means by 'God'. 'God is sacred' is true, because by 'sacred' is meant 'made holy by association with God'. And I venture to say that even the most ardent sceptic will admit that if there is a God, it is quite likely that He is in close association with Himself.

If doubt still lurks, if questions remain as to the logical status of the conclusion, then I suggest the following test: take the statement 'life is sacred' in this particular theological context, and see if it can be falsified. See if evidence, even in theory, can be found that would count against its truth. I think one would be hard pressed to find any. Notice that the problem of finding evidence is not merely a practical difficulty, but has an air of logical impossibility about it; for it makes about as much sense to look for empirical evidence to show that 'life is sacred' is false, as to look for evidence to show that 'seven plus five equals twelve' is false.

Edward Shils's notion of a protoreligious metaphysic is plagued by similar difficulties. According to Shils, 'the idea of sacredness is generated by the primordial experience of being alive, of experiencing the elemental sensation of vitality and the elemental fear of its extinction.'[8] The inviolability of human life is then self-evident, since it is 'the most primordial of experiences'.[9] But what, may I ask, would count as evidence against this claim? Approximately two hundred children in the United States die every year from lead poisoning because we are not greatly concerned about slum children – would this count as evidence? Again, as many as four hundred thousand children may be lead-poisoned, half of them ending up with permanent handicaps[10] – does this count? And what of the *conservative* estimate that as many as twenty-three thousand traffic fatalities in 1969 resulted from drunken driving? Or that cirrhosis is the sixth leading cause of death? Yet

[8] Edward Shils, op. cit., p. 12.
[9] Ibid., pp. 18–19.
[10] Margaret English, 'Lead Poisoned', *Look* Magazine, October 12, 1969, p. 114.

little or no fuss is made over the sale of alcoholic beverages. The American Cancer Society predicted in 1969 that lung cancer, which has been linked mostly to smoking, would kill more than fifty-one thousand men in the United States in the following year.[11] More recently, Nicholas Johnson (F.C.C. Commissioner) claimed that 'there are three hundred thousand deaths a year related to cigarette smoking'.[12] Nevertheless, the sale of cigarettes is still legal. If all this (and the surface has only been scratched) does not count against the self-evident status of the inviolability of human life, then what does count?

Shils evidently believes, first, that one must know the truth in order properly to recognize it; second, that those who do not have this prior understanding cannot see the truth, at least not as he conceives it; and third, that the reason people do not have this prior understanding is that they are morally misguided or obviously evil. He grudgingly admits that 'there is, in fact, no situation in which the acknowledgement of sanctity-of-life is guaranteed'.[13] Nonetheless, he insists on abusing those who would disagree with him, those who do not acknowledge the SLP. In more kindly moments, he dismisses those who do not agree as advocates of 'Prometheanism' or the prophets of what he calls 'contrived intervention'.[14] In a more revealing opening statement, he says that 'to persons who are not murderers, concentration camp administrators, or dreamers of sadistic fantasies, the inviolability of human life seems to be so self-evident that it might appear pointless to inquire into it'.[15] Evidently Shils believes that two opposing moral interpretations cannot be equally respectable, and that it is therefore necessary to condemn at least one of the interpreters as immoral.

Perhaps Shils was aware of these difficulties, for there is a shift in his position, an attempt to cover the empirical claim under the

---

[11] Nancy Hicks, 'Lung Cancer in Men Expected to Show Sharp Rise', *New York Times*, November 4, 1969.
[12] Nicholas Johnson, 'Dear President Agnew . . .', *The New York Times Theatre Section*, October 11, 1970, p. 17.
[13] Shils, op. cit., p. 18.
[14] Ibid., pp. 11–12.　　　　[15] Ibid., p. 2.

cloak of a normative one. In the same passage, where he maintains that the sacredness of life 'is the most primordial of experiences', and that 'the fact that many human beings act contrarily, or do not apprehend it, does not impugn the sacredness of life', he goes on to suggest that the proposition in question 'is no more than a guiding principle'. Surely, if it is no more than a guiding principle, no more than a normative principle, then it is not a natural metaphysic, it is not in the nature of things. If something is the case, then it makes little sense to say that we ought to make it so. If life is really sacred, then it makes little sense to say that it ought to be so treated. On the other hand, if there is nothing in the universe which necessitates or guarantees the sacredness of life, and if the claim is only that life *ought* to be treated as being sacred, then it makes even less sense to argue that there is a protoreligious natural metaphysic. Shils cannot have it both ways.

Some men are reluctant to talk in the first person, and are reluctant to say 'I think we ought to treat human beings in such and such a way', or 'I think we ought not to kill'. Instead they prefer to give their desires and preferences an impersonal sense of importance. Hence, we are told that cosmic forces, the gods, or some protoreligious metaphysic guarantees the efficacy of their desires. I believe it was Bertrand Russell who warned us that metaphysical ethics is an attempt to give universal rather than merely personal importance to certain of our desires. The ethical metaphysician believes that whatever he morally desires must (in some sense) exist and can be discovered in the ultimate nature of the universe. He confuses wishful thinking with fact. He rejects evidence for a sense of self-importance, and truth for the warmth of illusion.

Justice

Consider (2), the principle that one ought never to kill an innocent human being because such an act would be unjust. It raises special problems. The primary methodological difficulty is that of dispelling ambiguities and determining exactly what is being asserted by this principle. The primary ethical difficulty is that of co-ordinating different considerations of justice; for there is justice in the sense of giving an individual his due and nothing more, and there is justice in the sense of non-arbitrary, impartial treatment, namely, justice as fairness.

For example, consider the problem of euthanasia : Are we giving patients their due when, with their consent, we allow them to die? Are we giving them their due when, with their consent, we kill those who suffer from incurable disease? And, in the wider sense of justice as fairness, is it fair to kill or to allow these patients to die? Few questions generate more difficulties for the advocates of the SLP, for there are few moral situations that raise more stubborn problems than the plight of a person who wants an easy and merciful death.

Perhaps the first point that strikes us when we reflect upon the problem is that (2) is not synonymous, and should not be confused, with :

(5) One ought not to kill an innocent human being because such an act would be breaking some code of law.

To say that we do not mean by 'justice' merely 'conformity to a code of law' is to utter an obvious truth about the language. But I think the point can be made more strongly. Not only do we not talk this way; there are good reasons why we ought not to. For once having equated justice with some code of law, consistency would demand that we call all laws just, even one that established the most vicious forms of inequity or led to untold human misery. Moreover, having essentially eliminated the term 'justice', we would probably want to introduce another term with an almost identical meaning in order to refer to unjust acts which are neither referred to nor covered by a code of law.

Now, one of the more popular objections to euthanasia is that :

(6) One ought not to commit an act of euthanasia because such an act would be illegal.

In normal times this is not a convincing argument. But in times when there is an almost hysterical demand for law and order, the argument gains a certain plausibility. The explanation usually given is that one is obligated to obey the law, and obedience to law is a prior and overriding moral commitment. If the issue is pressed further and one asks : 'Would you feel the same obligation if you were, let us say, in Nazi Germany?', there are a variety of replies. But more often than not we are told that while there is a prior obligation to obey the law, this does not and cannot make it right to inflict or obey a harmful law. The reply, in itself, is not decisive, but it does illustrate the fact that advocates and opponents of euthanasia often agree that some rules are overriding, and that prior obligations do not make it right to inflict or obey harmful laws, generally speaking.[16]

A more serious objection to euthanasia is that :

(7) One ought not to commit an act of euthanasia because it is unjust in the sense of punishing someone when no punishment is due.

Thus we are told that a patient is usually not guilty of a crime – that he is innocent – and that to punish him by killing is unjust.[17]

For example, suppose we have a case of disseminated carcinoma metastasis before us – that is, a case of cancer where the cancerous cells have spread and have fully developed throughout the body. We know that the patient suffers excruciating pain; that as a result of this condition it is beyond reasonable medical

---

[16] There is an added proviso to this, namely, that in cases of conflict this rule should yield to the principle of suffering – that it is always wrong to cause unnecessary suffering. Hence in cases where this rule conflicts with the aforementioned principle, the decision-making process should be more complex than that suggested above.

[17] A similar argument is used to support the claim that euthanasia is not merciful. For a reply, see pp. 72–76, 94–5.

doubt that the patient has to die; that the patient has earlier completed a 'living will'[18] and when told of his condition voluntarily favours some means of 'easy death'; and that aside from the desire to help the patient no other considerations are relevant. Now it is not easy to know all these things, and I am not suggesting that it is. What I am suggesting is that if there are such cases (and I believe there are), then in these cases it would not be unjust to kill.

Some would disagree with this analysis. The question is, why? One source of the difficulty lies in the belief that death is and always must be considered to be a punishment. This belief has various sources: the notion that immortality is a necessary condition for perfection, the belief that God punished man by expelling him from the Garden of Eden (thereby making him mortal), and the fact that human beings almost universally use death as an extreme form of punishment. Given all this, it is easy to understand why people view death as punishment.

The significant question is not whether human beings have certain prejudices, as admittedly they do, but whether in the situation described the act of killing is really a punishment. The evidence indicates that the intention is not to inflict pain, restraint, or any other penalty. Moreover, the patient himself does not view it as punishment. On the contrary, he wants to die. In fact, the patient might argue that his having a 'living will' places an obligation on his physician and family. Now, the question of contract is a moot one. Morally, much depends upon the nature and extent of the promises made by the family, while legally the matter is even more complex. But what is eminently clear is that in such situations the patient – if he is not actually demanding death as a matter of equity – certainly does not view it as punishment or inequity. Without contrary evidence, dogmatically to

[18] *A Living Will*, prepared and printed by the Euthanasia Educational Fund, 1969, reprinted 1970. 'A form to be filled out by a person of sound mind and after careful consideration, indicating to his family, physician, clergyman and lawyer, his wishes in case of his own incapacity or terminal illness.' See also the 'Form of Declaration' given in the appendix of *Euthanasia and the Right to Death*, op. cit.

assert in the face of this that all death is punishment is to be like a man who, after carefully examining a black swan, refuses to call it such, because he was taught to believe that all swans are white.

I should now like to consider what is at best a moral anomaly; *result of careless thinking* that is, the belief that euthanasia is merciful, but nonetheless unjust. The anomaly is the result of careless thinking, of essentially identifying the concept of being *not just* with that of being *unjust*. While the belief in its pure form is not widely held, something very much like it keeps cropping up in lay discussions.

The belief is that :

(8) One ought not to commit an act of euthanasia because, although it is merciful, merciful acts are somehow unjust.

The temptation is to reduce this 'argument' to absurdity by showing that if the position is consistently held, all merciful acts – including the merciful treatment of criminals and unfortunate victims of war and oppression, and even the merciful acts of a deity – must be considered unjust. This temptation should be resisted, however, not because it is mistaken, but because such a manœuvre explains little and tends to veil the underlying problems.

I think that once this view is clearly stated, it will be generally rejected. It will not be accepted that all acts are either just or unjust, since it is generally recognized that a narrow notion of equity is applicable only in those situations where such a notion is relevant as an issue. For example, given this narrow sense of justice it seems exceedingly odd to say that an act – such as the act of making a charitable donation in circumstances where it is not a matter of obligation – is either just or unjust. Clearly, in this circumstance it is only a matter of benevolence. Again, consider the phenomenon of self-sacrifice. Take a case in which a stranger gives his own life in an attempt to help the unfortunate victims in a burning house. Surely, without additional information that would alter our understanding of the situation, there is something bizarre in saying that the act was unjust because the victims did not deserve the treatment they received.

Nor can we accept the tacit assumption that morality is synonymous with this narrow view of equity. Even if we maintain that justice requires equal treatment in all essentially similar cases, and further hold that this broader notion of equity is somehow synonymous with morality, the claim that one ought to give everyone his due and *nothing more* cannot stand up under critical scrutiny. It cannot stand because justice is not a miser. Justice may demand impartiality in the observance or enforcement of certain rules of distribution,[19] but she does not require that we only distribute goods and services on the basis of a previous contract. She does not reduce morality to a niggardly form of obligation.

Consequentialist Arguments

The arguments I shall now consider grow out of the feeling, often an unshakeable conviction, that the SLP is necessary because its violation leads to undesirable consequences. Norman St John-Stevas maintains that 'once the principle of the sanctity-of-life is abandoned, there can be no criterion of the right to life, save that of personal taste'.[20] Edward Shils makes a stronger claim, stating that 'if life were not viewed and experienced as sacred, then nothing else would be sacred'.[21] Although there is difference of opinion as to exactly what the violation entails, it is generally agreed that :

> (3) One ought never to kill an innocent human being because such an action may (or must) lead to undesirable consequences.

[19] Henry Sidgwick, *The Methods of Ethics*, 2nd ed. (London: Macmillan, 1877), p. 263.
[20] Norman St John-Stevas, op. cit., p. 17.
[21] Edward Shils, op. cit., pp. 14–15.

Consider the most vulnerable form of this argument. Here it is claimed that :

(9) One ought never to kill an innocent human being because such an action *may* lead to undesirable consequences.

Now, many argue that (9) must be rejected. They maintain, and correctly so, that in a democracy misuse or abuse of law is almost a necessary correlate, since in a free society one cannot make laws strong enough to repress possible violations. Hence it is a serious mistake to expect perfect regulation and still cherish the values of liberty. Others say that the argument must be rejected because its underlying form is such that it can be used to oppose all political and social change on the grounds that there is always a possibility of abuse, and that (9) and similar arguments are merely clandestine defences of the status quo; that is to say, little more than apologetics for present suffering and misery. Others go further and make a distinction between the appeal to consequences and the demand for moral perfection. The former is legitimate. A rational man must consider the consequences of his actions. But the latter, the demand for moral perfection, is unreasonable.

Aside from these pragmatic considerations, there is a logical objection that is, I believe, telling. If the only constraint is logical impossibility, then it is just as possible that an action *will not* have undesirable consequences. The result is a complete stalemate. For if it is equally as possible to have desirable as to have undesirable consequences, then an appeal to such consequences is completely indecisive and the argument breaks down. The argument is of little value except, perhaps, to point out that actions do have consequences.

It is interesting to note that opponents of euthanasia use a similar argument. They maintain that if euthanasia is legalized, or even held to be moral, then all sorts of disastrous consequences may follow. We reply that it is equally possible that it may not be abused. Logically speaking, the point is telling. Unfortunately, however, it is not persuasive. Following Joseph Fletcher, we then ask : 'What is more irresponsible than to hide . . . behind a logical possibility that is without antecedent probability ?'[22] Again, the point is telling, and again, the opponents of euthanasia are not persuaded. The question is, why not?

By way of explanation, I should like to advance two conjectures. The more obvious is that the notion of logical possibility is unclear, or is being run together with other notions. Therefore, it may be worthwhile to see if the boundaries of this notion can be more properly illuminated.

The only constraint upon logical possibility is that of logical impossibility, i.e., everything not logically impossible is logically possible. Now, the only logically impossible 'things' are those events, acts, and so forth, that if expressed in language result in a contradictory sentence.[23] For example, we say that it is not logically possible for a material object to be black and not black at the same time and place, because we know that the sentence, 'The black object is not a black object' is contradictory. Since logical impossibility is an extremely limited kind of constraint, however, it neither marks off nor prohibits unconfirmable, false, or conjectural sentences. Hence, one can say with equal impunity that the black object may transubstantiate itself into a vampire bat, or that it may not; that the man may run the mile in two minutes, or that he may not; and that euthanasia may lead to abuse, or that it may not.

The other explanation is that (9) is not as simple as it seems to be, because an important facet of the argument has been omitted. Perhaps they mean to say that the practice of euthanasia may lead to abuse, and if it does, then the quality of the abuse

---

[22] Joseph Fletcher, 'Elective Death', in *Ethical Issues in Medicine*, ed. E. F. Torrey (Boston: Little, Brown & Co., 1968), p. 145.

[23] A contradictory sentence is a simple sentence in which the predicate term is the precise denial of the subject term. For a more adequate characterization of a fully contradictory sentence, see: Jerrold J. Katz, *The Philosophy of Language* (London and New York: Harper & Row, 1966), p. 198.

outweighs the quality of its non-abuse, and that this is unfair. Here, I think, one has to be careful not to muddle two different problems. The first is the problem of appealing to possible consequences without any supporting evidence. The second is the problem of appealing to possible consequences with the support of evidence. To be more specific, we are now being told that:

(10) One ought never to make euthanasia permissible, because there is evidence that people who ought not to die will die, and that this is unfair.

This, however, differs significantly from the claim that one ought never to make euthanasia permissible, because it may lead to undesirable consequences.

Concerning (10) and the question of fairness, I would agree that one should ask: is it fair that people who ought not to, will die because of mistakes and abuses? But fairness is a double-edged sword. One must also ask: is it fair that those who ought to die will not be allowed to do so? Better yet: is it fairer to prevent the many who ought to die from doing so in order to protect the few who ought not to? And at what point does one draw the line? Would it be fairer to let one thousand, ten thousand, or one hundred thousand suffer in order to prevent the unjust death of, let us say, one man?

This is a difficult and heart-rending question. I know of no easy answer. But it seems almost self-evident that if the criterion is to be fairness, then fairness demands that we examine and weigh both sides. Moreover, if the criterion is to be fairness, and someone must pay the piper, then the very best we can do is to minimize and distribute equitably the unfairness.

I now turn to the consequentialist argument which has the greatest intuitive appeal, namely, that:

(11) One ought never to kill an innocent human being because such an action *must* lead to undesirable consequences.

There are many varieties of this argument, but I shall only consider what I believe to be its most compelling forms:

(11 : 1) One ought never to kill an innocent human being because such an action must lead to a universal contempt for all life.

(11 : 2) One must never sanction the practice of euthanasia because such an action must lead to the killing of the chronically ill, the senile, the mentally defective, the socially unproductive, and/or the ideologically unwanted.

As to (11 : 1), here the forgotten hero is Albert Schweitzer, for, unlike most moralists, Schweitzer insists that the principle of reverence for life is universal in scope. Whenever possible, no living thing should be killed.[24]

To the truly ethical man, all life is sacred, including forms of life that from the human point of view may seem to be lower than ours.[25]

A man is truly ethical only when he obeys the compulsion to help all life which he is able to assist, and shrinks from injuring anything that lives. He does not ask how far this or that life deserves one's sympathy as being valuable, nor, beyond that, whether and to what degree it is capable of feeling. Life as such is sacred to him. He tears no leaf from a tree, plucks no flower, and takes care to crush no insect. If in summer he is working by lamplight, he prefers to keep the window shut and breathe a stuffy atmosphere than see

[24] The principle of reverence for life says that, generally speaking, one ought not to kill anything, and that the principle of not-killing 'must be the servant of, and subordinate itself to, compassion'; moreover, there are times when we are forced to decide which life we will sacrifice in order to preserve other lives. See: Schweitzer, *Indian Thought and Its Development* (London: A. & C. Black, 1967; Boston: Beacon Press, 1960), pp. 83–84; *The Teaching of Reverence for Life* (London: Peter Owen, 1966; New York: Holt, Rinehart and Winston, 1965), pp. 47–49.
[25] *The Teaching of Reverence for Life*, p. 47.

one insect after another fall with singed wings upon his table.[26]

Schweitzer's work is seldom referred to by advocates of the SLP. At first I thought this was merely an oversight, but I suspect that there is more to it than that. If the idea of killing[27] is in itself contagious (which seems to be the shared underlying premise), then why stop at the idea of killing human beings? If it is contagious, then surely the idea of killing any living being is just as contagious, and Schweitzer's conclusion follows. But non-Schweitzerians are reluctant to draw this conclusion. Perhaps they recognize the danger. Perhaps they sense that his interpretation cannot stand, and that if Schweitzer's can't, theirs can't.

The basic issue is whether or not the idea of killing is contagious – that is, whether or not a person, group or society exposed to actual killing, or the idea of sanctioned killing, universalizes and thereby extends this domain. I maintain that this question is best answered in the negative; that there is overwhelming evidence indicating that human beings compartmentalize their experience and ideas; and that it is only when the normal process of compartmentalization breaks down that one encounters difficulties.

This does not mean that human beings don't generalize. But it does mean that in the normal process of generalization there are constraints, and one of the more important constraints is that the process is limited by the concept of 'same kind or same class of objects'. For example, if we crush an insect and believe this to be a permissible act, we do not conclude that it is permissible to kill all living things. We conclude only that it is permissible to kill that kind of insect, or at most, all kinds of insects. Similarly, if we are taught to kill Nazis and the criteria for a Nazi and the

[26] Albert Schweitzer, *The Philosophy of Civilization* (London: A. & C. Black, 1946; New York: Macmillan, 1960), p. 310.
[27] It is not exactly clear what the relation is between having the idea and actually killing, but the literature assumes that there is a direct causal relation. Whether this is true or not is another matter, and one that should be more carefully explored.

B

circumstances of permissible killing are clearly spelled out, we do not kill all German nationals (although of the possible mistakes this is probably the most likely). We do not mistakenly generalize and kill all Europeans. Nor do we proceed either in fact or in mind to kill all human beings.

In other words, (11) and its cognates share a common premise, and I am urging that that premise is not true. The evidence indicates that the killing of human beings in 'X' situations does not necessarily lead to the killing of human beings in non-'X' situations. Or, to be more concrete, the merciful killing of patients who want to die does not necessarily lead to the killing of the unwanted or the extermination of the human species. I believe that this is true; but I would like to add that my beliefs are not synonymous with truth. I may be mistaken. For the question at issue is not one of beliefs, nor is it a matter of metaphysical mystagogy. It is a question of fact, and one that needs to be more fully explored by social scientists.

Questions of Ultimacy and Supremacy

Various interpretations of the sanctity-of-life principle have been examined, but thus far we have only considered those which admit or provide grounds for validation. There are other interpretations which do not possess this characteristic, and we would not be doing justice to them if we did not consider at least one other claim, namely, that :

(4) The sentence 'One ought never to kill an innocent human being' expresses an ultimate moral principle.

In order to understand this claim, a fundamental distinction, often badly neglected or blurred beyond recognition, must now be drawn : when we speak of an 'ultimate principle' we may, within a given theory, be referring to that characteristic whereby the principle is the final arbiter of any conflict of values. On the other hand, we may be referring to that characteristic whereby the principle in question cannot be reduced to, or justified by an appeal to, other rules or principles. In the first case, the case of 'ultimate₁', the word is held to be partially synonymous with the word 'supreme'; in the case of 'ultimate₂', there is an overlap with the meaning of the word 'primitive'.

Given sentence-type (4) and the existence of this ambiguity, the following may be obtained:

(12) The sentence 'One ought never to kill an innocent human being' expresses a supreme (ultimate₁) moral principle, a principle that is the final arbiter.

(13) The sentence 'One ought never to kill an innocent human being' expresses an ultimate (ultimate₂) moral principle, a principle that cannot be reduced to, or justified by an appeal to, other rules or principles.

As to (13), it is a truism to say that ultimate principles are ultimate. Similarly, it is true, but not very enlightening, to say that if a principle in a given theory is held to be the ultimate validating principle, then it is held to be ultimate. A more interesting internal question is whether the purported principle is actually the one that is held to be ultimate. That is to say, is the notion of 'not killing' the ultimate validating principle here?

By way of reply, first notice that the word 'innocent' is included in this formulation. Notice also that this implies that what is ultimate is some principle of justice, and not the notion of not killing. For if the ultimate constraint is that of protecting the innocent, then it seems to follow that the ultimate validating principle is one of justice.

It may be charged that (13) is a 'loaded' formulation. I agree. But I am curious to know what other formulation would be better. Is it better to delete the word 'innocent' and suggest that it is never permissible to kill a human being? Or, in the linguistic mode, to maintain that:

(14) The sentence 'One ought never to kill a human being'
is an ultimate moral principle.

Perhaps. At least it reflects the sincere belief that human life
should be placed above all other considerations and that it is
never right to kill a human being. To reply by saying, quite
correctly, that neither the major religions nor the general literature assumes such a position, is not relevant (although it does
indicate the direction in which the general sentiment lies).
However, other objections, which turn on the problem of self-
defence and the dubious distinction between allowing oneself to
be killed by another person and directly killing (which would be
inconsistent), are not so easily met. Suffice it to say that if the
choice is between (13) and (14), then either one has to accept
the fact that (13) is not an ultimate principle, or one must accept
the consequences of (14).

As to (12), here we turn to the heart of the matter: namely,
the belief that the prohibition of killing is the supreme moral
principle, and that as such it is overriding, the final arbiter. The
question I wish to raise is, why the prohibition of killing and not
some other principle?

There is something systematically misleading in talking about
principles rather than rules. But if one insists on talking in the
language of principles, if the existence of conflicting principles
is a fact of moral life, and if intelligent men advance and support
different principles, why should we choose this one? Why the
SLP? It will not do to say that the truth of the matter is self-
evident. This not only begs the question, but ignores overwhelming evidence. Nor will it do to claim that all ultimate principles
are supreme, for this muddles different characteristics.

Instead of (12), why not say that one should always act with
love? Why not say that in some situations love demands that we
kill? If it be objected that a love ethic is too fulfilling, or that to
act lovingly is to exceed the demands of morality, then the reply
is disarmingly simple. If the love ethic is too broad (too rich,
which it seems to be), and the vitalistic ethic too narrow (too poor,

which it seems to be), then if one must make a choice, the love ethic is better, since it is at least rich enough to account for the wide diversity of moral experience.

However, I do not wish to give the impression that the love principle is the only one that can be successfully matched against the SLP. Indeed, I have repeatedly maintained that there are times when one ought to kill because killing is the kindest possible thing we can do. This would follow from a love ethic, but it also follows from the rule of benevolence. The rule of benevolence says that :

> We owe to all men such services as we can render by a sacrifice or effort small in comparison with the service : and hence, in proportion as the needs of other men present themselves are urgent, we recognize the duty of relieving them out of superfluity.[28]

The rule suggests that we ought to be kind; that, where we can, we ought to help those who are in need or distress.

The rule of benevolence has its share of difficulties – the problem of justification, the problem of explicating the meaning of the word 'benevolence', the problem of how to determine the consequences of an action, and so forth. Nonetheless, much can be said for the other side of the ledger. Even though it is difficult to do, rationality demands that we consider the consequences of a proposed act. Admittedly, the notion of benevolence is difficult to explicate. But I think it is also true that, as compared to more obscure notions like 'The Good', it is easier – note that I did not say 'easy' – to reach agreement as to when people are suffering, and as to what would relieve their suffering.[29]

[28] Henry Sidgwick, op. cit., p. 232.
[29] I am indebted to Karl Popper for a similar point.

2

What is Moral Killing?

In this chapter I wish to do three things. First, I wish to suggest that much of the intellectual frustration encountered in discussions on the morality of killing is due to unrealistic expectations as to what a theory of killing can do. I shall then briefly examine what is probably the strongest version or interpretation of the absolutist claim that one ought never to kill an innocent human being. Finally, after reconstructing the sanctity-of-life principle, I shall attempt to do the same for the notion of self-defence, and thereby, tacitly defend the thesis that all killing in self-defence is justifiable homicide.

I

It is often maintained that the problem of moral killing is not solvable. Numerous reasons are advanced. Perhaps the simplest is the claim of the ordinary man that the problem is not solvable because disagreement is always possible. To which the obvious reply is that, if free dissent includes the possibility of being unreasonable, then dissent in itself is not a decisive factor. But the argument might be put thus : there is something about the nature of this problem that precludes the possibility of obtaining consensus even among rational men. Admittedly, there is an element of truth here. Yet some emendation is necessary. Let us say that there is something about this problem, and perhaps about the nature of all basic moral problems, that makes it extremely difficult to obtain consensus. But, aside perhaps from the public subjectivist, who would want to maintain seriously that agreement is the sole answer to a moral dilemma? Unless, of course, the dilemma is that of achieving agreement.

To my mind the most telling of the 'no solution' approaches is to argue that there is no objective solution because all genuinely moral statements are optatives. The term 'optative', I should add, refers to any sentence that is expressive of a wish, a proposal, a prohibition, or the like, whether or not it also contains meaning components referring to matters of fact. An expanded version of the argument is that, since optatives require further optatives as their justification, the choice is either an infinite regression or the postulation of higher, perhaps ultimate, principles. Now there is little to be gained from quibbling over the various senses of the word 'objective'. What is important to note is that as a non-cognitivist one need neither argue that there is no solution nor attempt to prohibit inquiry in this area. The contention, which I share, would be that moral inquiry is limited, two of the most important factors being the optative nature of moral statements, and that optatives differ from non-optatives in their mode of justification. To put this differently : just as it is unrealistic to expect a proposed solution to thwart unreasonable doubt, it is almost equally unrealistic to expect solutions of moral problems to match moves which are only feasible in the more cognitive areas of human endeavour.

The central question is, what set of meta-criteria generates a more adequate theory?

The following criteria are proposed. Aside from the usual cognitive desiderata (clarity, consistency, maximum scope, and warranted assertability), a theory of killing must (1) provide information which enables us reasonably to decide when it is and when it is not moral to kill. (2) A theory must be consistent with the basic principles of morality. That is, consistent with at least two basic and independent principles, that of need utility (which tells us to minimize human misery and those conditions which interfere with the satisfaction of basic needs), and that of justice. (3) Other things being equal, one theory is better than another to the extent that it provides criteria (a) which are clear and self-sufficient, and (b) which enable actors to make judgments both in paradigm-like and novel situations. By 'self-sufficient' here is meant 'not solely dependent upon an appeal to authority'. The notion of having a rule which applies to novel situations is, perhaps, best illustrated by way of analogy. Consider the difference between the rule that 'one ought not to make open fires in bedrooms', and the rule that 'open fires ought not to be made in places where it is reasonable to believe the fire will get out of hand'. The former is paradigm-like; the latter applies to this situation, as well as to novel ones.

I would not want the foregoing to be confused with other entirely different attempts to produce sufficient conditions, or to provide ultimate principles (ultimate in the sense of not being open to further discussion or justification). Not only are the conditions described above minimal, but discussion in this area is very much needed, and emendations should be made where necessary.

II

If we survey the development of the principles of moral killing, we frequently find that they are hinted at, or expressed, in terms of the principles of sanctity-of-life and self-defence. The former tells us when not to kill; the latter when it is permissible.

What I propose to do here is to examine what for many seems to be the most viable form of the sanctity-of-life principle, namely, the absolutist claim that 'one ought never to kill an innocent human being'.

1. KILLING

Killing is almost always viewed negatively as the taking of life. The weight of the injunction is against deliberate killing. To do otherwise, to declare, for example, that one ought never accidentally to kill has the absurd ring of morally prohibiting accidents. Moral philosophers also distinguish between allowing and causing death. Killing is synonymous with the latter. That is, to be an act of killing an act must cause death directly and imminently.

2. HUMAN BEING

There seems to be an unusual amount of disagreement on this point. Nonetheless, many absolutists believe the only viable option is to maintain that, from the moment of conception, the foetus of human parents and all other members of the species *homo sapiens* are human beings. For this, in their opinion, affords the greatest protection for the greatest number.

3. NEVER

Most of us are inclined to believe that typically one ought not to kill innocent human beings. We believe this either in itself, or as a corollary of other moral principles, the most obvious of which is the principle of justice. The absolutist, however, goes a step further. His claim is not that typically or generally one ought not to kill, but that the killing of the innocent is *never* directly permissible. 'It is in no way lawful to slay the innocent.'[1]

To kill the innocent, we are told, is to punish unfairly. It is to impart a determination of evil, and this can never be done justly. As an explanation this has a ring of truth. More often than not, to kill the innocent is to punish. But this is not always the case. How many of us have had to kill or help kill human beings that we truly loved? Are cases of beneficent euthanasia cases of punishment? I think not. Perhaps it is a mistake to try to be merciful in a seemingly merciless universe. But how, and by what stretch of logic, can either the intention or actual act be considered to be punishment? By what sophistry does one decide that kind treatment (perhaps the kindest possible) is necessarily an act of punishment?

To say that killing the innocent imparts a determination of evil, and that this can never be done justly, raises other difficulties. John Hersey, in his novel *The Wall*, tells the story of Isaac, a six-month-old child who is killed by a resistance leader in order

---

[1] St Thomas Aquinas, *Summa Theologica*, 2.2.64.6. '. . . The innocent and righteous slay thou not.' *Exodus* 23 : 7.

to save the lives of approximately ninety people. The child is certainly not guilty of breaking any law. If it may be construed as a mistake, his mistake was to refuse to stop crying when German troops approached the bunker on a search-and-destroy mission. Was the killing of Isaac done justly or unjustly? Suppose we reply by saying that it was done justly. This entails that the killing of the innocent can be just even if such cases are extremely rare. But suppose we take the opposite view. After all, not killing Isaac allows the Germans to kill the others, and this is not the same as being responsible for the direct killing of all the Jews in the bunker. But this also entails a so-called moral principle: that it is just to allow many innocent human beings to die when, by acting otherwise, one could have reasonably prevented their deaths. Perhaps as a principle of prudence, that whatever the moral consequences, one ought to keep one's hands as morally clean as possible, the latter gains an air of plausibility. But as a principle of justice it is patently absurd.

4. INNOCENT

The question is, in what sense of the word 'innocent' is it true to say that one ought not to kill?

Most theologians, and the legal tradition that follows, maintain that being innocent is a matter of not being guilty of violating rules or laws. There are several reasons for this. First, there is the belief that the revealed will of God is the sole source of all moral legislation, and that consequently every punishable act constitutes a sin, a violation of God's will. Second, the wilful commission of sin is considered a deliberate rejection of the authority of God, a denial in word or deed of guilt. In short, a man is innocent only if he is not guilty of violating God's law. Parallel to this is the secular position which argues that, whatever be the source of morality, certain laws accurately reflect this, and a man is held to be innocent only if he is not guilty of violation. Finally, and theology aside, it is generally held that it is best to make moral judgments on the basis of an established body of law. One reason for this is that it guarantees a high level of stability, and thereby avoids the dangers of subjectivism, or what is worse, the more pernicious forms of anarchy. Another is that the intellect of ordinary human beings is hampered by the impulses of the senses and the imagination, and is thereby very prone to error. Still another is that, given the self-centredness and short-sightedness of ordinary human nature or character, the danger of abuse is so great that, as a practical rule of moral conduct, the sanctity-of-life principle should be kept inviolate and the determination of guilt should be essentially in the hands of proper moral authorities; for this is the only practical defence against abuse.[2]

Apparently, most of us are intellectually and morally fallible; others are not. Those who are, have to be deceived, or at least deluded into believing the principle is inviolable and that the appeal to authority is the only proper way of determining guilt.

Suppose the worst to be true. Suppose the masses are morally careless, even decadent, and the elite morally pure. What follows from this? I suspect very little. If ordinary human nature, and not human nature *per se*, is morally fallible then the answer lies in education. If, on the other hand, human nature itself is at fault, then there are several options, the most drastic being that of eugenics. But whatever the best strategy may be, it seems eminently clear that a form of moral authoritarianism is one of the worst alternatives. More important, the promulgation of the principle on the basis of deliberate deceit is nothing but unadulterated fraud. And, I am very much tempted to say, it is never possible to achieve a moral end by deceit or fraud. But this is not true, unfortunately. Some ends can be achieved in that manner. Nonetheless, I am constrained to believe that we cannot have intellectual dishonesty of such magnitude and an adequate general moral condition. Fraud cannot sustain the good life.

Although these are important considerations, I do not wish to give the impression that there are no cognitive difficulties. Quite the contrary. To say that someone is innocent$_1$, i.e., not

---

[2] I am indebted to W. Norris Clarke for bringing a similar argument to my attention.

guilty of violating certain rules or laws, is almost vacuous. Although this sense of the word may be useful, it does not 'wear the pants'. Rather, it is a 'tell us where to look for an answer' sense of the word.

The word 'innocent' has another important sense. We often say that X is innocent$_2$ if X's existence or actions neither have caused nor will cause imminent harm. Similarly, we sometimes say that being innocent$_{2a}$ means not being a member of a group whose collective or combined activities are harmful.[3] Indeed, to say 'X is innocent' will, unless the context points explicitly in other directions, imply or suggest that X is not guilty of injuring others.

My proposal is that the sanctity-of-life principle be reformulated. First, it should be interpreted as a rule, a rule which would not apply to cases of beneficent euthanasia; and second, the word 'innocent' (in this context) should always be interpreted to mean 'innocent$_2$'. Given these changes we obtain the principle that, generally speaking, one ought not to kill a human being whose existence or actions neither have caused nor will cause imminent harm.

The truth is, of course, that this formulation has advantages and disadvantages. Probably the most serious disadvantage is that in the search for a more objective norm it has been necessary to introduce the notion of imminent harm. The application of this notion will, no doubt, lead to difficulties or possible abuse. Yet, aside from cognates such as 'misery' or 'suffering', one would be hard pressed to find a basic value term which would generate less difficulty.

There are also advantages which seem to more than balance out the disadvantages. First, the reconstructed principle (unlike its predecessor) provides criteria (a) which are reasonably clear and self-sufficient, and (b) which enable actors to make judgments both in paradigm-like and novel situations. Second, since it covers both intentional and un- (or non-) intentional deeds, it has greater scope; for we can now talk more plausibly about the

[3] I am indebted to Michael Walzer for this point.

possible guilt of foetuses, groups, and institutions. Third, the avoidance of imminent harm which is here implied is an important (though not the chief) part of the principle of need utility. Fourth, the idea that innocence should depend, in this context, solely upon effects is consistent with the utilitarian doctrine (and moral intuition) that the rightness of actions is to be judged by their consequences. Finally, by urging that we treat entities who intend no harm but who, nonetheless, cause harm as being guilty,[4] the reconstructed principle is in full accord with the idea that it is just to protect ourselves against harm. Moreover, it avoids the absurdity of having to say that it is better to allow a thousand or even a million innocent human beings to die than to kill one innocent person.

III

The sanctity-of-life principle tells us when one ought not to kill. It does not, however, tell us when one is entitled or when it is permissible to kill. Now it would be morally gross to assume that one is entitled to kill all those who are not innocent. Another principle is needed, one which can serve as an effective complement. Here the most likely candidate is the principle of self-defence. And the question I wish to focus upon is, what exactly are we protecting when we say we have the right to use force, if necessary deadly force, to protect a person or group against imminent harm, especially irreparable injury?

Except by certain pacifists, it is agreed that we at least have the right to protect life. One might be inclined to believe this simply means that if an individual is physically assaulted, he is entitled to protect himself against harm. But this does not seem to be the case. Qualification, often several qualifications, are added.

In Canon Law, for example, defence is legitimate against an unjust aggressor only if due moderation is observed. The latter,

---

[4] Since they are not belligerents, it would be a mistake to call them aggressors, whether they be unjust or not.

that it is essential that no more force be used than the occasion necessitates, is usually interpreted to mean that a homicide caused by unlawful force is unlawful. The qualification, on the surface, seems to be reasonable enough. If circumstances warrant it and one can, one ought to retreat and avoid violence. One ought not to overreact. One ought not to kill unnecessarily. I suspect that this qualification is based upon a minimization principle, the principle that one ought to avoid causing any unnecessary suffering. If this is correct, then the right to protect life (and presumably all rights guaranteed by the principle of self-defence) are so restricted.

On the level of theory this seems well and good. But in practical situations it is often unreasonable to expect those who are being attacked to know what an assailant's intentions are. For example, the victim of a thief who is threatened with his life and robbed may not know that the weapon in question is merely a harmless replica. In this situation the victim may reasonably believe that he must physically disable his assailant – the supposition being that, if the victim reasonably believes his life is in danger, he has the right to protect himself, and if necessary the right to kill. Hence, the test as to the extent of justification is neither knowing nor merely believing. The test is whether the person reasonably believes the force he proposes to use is necessary.[5]

A crucial question is, what constitutes reasonable belief? One might be tempted to say that the question need not be answered, at least not from a practical point of view. All that is necessary, it might be suggested, is that whatever judgment the assaultee makes, it be consistent with the judgment, the intuitive judgment of a possible jury. Like most appeals to intuition this presupposes criteria, but fails to explicate them. How would the jury know

---

[5] Given these conditions almost any homicide may be justified, even those which would normally be considered outrageous, such as patricide. For an interesting case of legally justifiable patricide, see: *Regina v. Cadwallander*, (1966). 1 C.C.C. 380; Saskatchewan Queen's Bench, which is described at length in M. L. Friedland, *Cases and Materials on Criminal Law and Procedure* (Toronto: University of Toronto Press, 1968; London: 1971), pp. 355–357.

what to decide? Or more generally, how does an individual or a group rationally decide it is reasonable to believe that it is being attacked, or that the intended preventive force is not excessive? Surely, these questions warrant further investigation, and, where possible, answers.

Aside from life, what other things do human beings have the right to protect? Here there seems to be a significant difference of opinion. In many societies it was, and in some it is still, lawful to defend life, property, and honour. 'Even where polite society has outlawed physical violence it retains the ritual slap on the face as a challenge to settle an affair of honour, and it was commonly admitted that offences to honour could only be redeemed through blood. "La lessive de l'honneur ne se coule qu'au sang." '[6] 'According to the accepted teaching of theologians,' writes Delany, 'it is lawful, in the defence of life or limb, of property of some importance, and of chastity, to repel violence with violence, even to the extent of killing an unjust assailant.'[7] In English Law a homicide is lawful if (but not only if) it is committed 'in reasonable self-defence of person or property or in order to prevent the commission of an atrocious crime.'[8] More recently, in a promulgated 'penal' code, it has been suggested that 'a person is privileged to threaten or intentionally use force against another for the purpose of preventing or terminating what he reasonably believes to be an unlawful interference with his person by such other person.'[9] Two observations are directly relevant : first, that in this section 'unlawful' means either tortious or expressly prohibited by criminal law or both, and second, that

[6] Julian Pitt-Rivers, 'Honour and Social Status' in *Honour and Shame: The Values of Mediterranean Society*, ed. J. G. Peristiany (London : Weidenfeld & Nicolson, 1966; Chicago: University of Chicago Press, 2nd imp., 1970), p. 25. The translated French reads: 'The laundry of honour is only bleached with blood.'
[7] Joseph F. Delany, 'Aggressor, Unjust', in *The Catholic Encyclopaedia*, ed. C. G. Hevermonne *et al.* (New York : Gilmary Society, 1907), Vol. 1.
[8] Rupert Cross and Philip Asterly Jones, *An Introduction to Criminal Law* (London : Butterworth, 1964), p. 130.
[9] Richard C. Donnelly, Joseph Goldstein and Richard D. Schwartz, *Criminal Law* (London : Collier Macmillan Ltd., 1963), p. 662.

the authors maintain that 'it is not reasonable to intentionally use force intended or likely to cause death or great bodily harm for the sole purpose of defence of one's property'.[10]

This brief review reveals that if the question is, what have people *believed* they have the right to protect, then the answer is almost anything they consider to have great value. The general belief seems to have been, and most of humanity probably still believes, that we have a right to kill to protect the things we value highly or cherish. This may include life, property, honour and even chastity. Nor does this list include, or have we mentioned thus far, the right to defend liberty, religion, moral principles, mental well-being or general well-being. Of course, there is a seemingly easy way out. We can follow Messrs Donnelly, Goldstein and Schwartz and formulate a principle that only sanctions defence against unlawful acts. The advantages of such a move are clear. On the one hand one avoids fossilizing antiquated moral beliefs, and on the other the law is allowed greater flexibility. The difficulty is that, although this version is better, it purports to solve the decision-making problem by shifting the burden onto the legislator. Similarly, one may be tempted to say that every society has the right to choose what it wishes to cherish, and the corresponding right to decide to protect the objects of its choice, if necessary by the use of deadly force. But even if this were true, there is still the larger question of what and how ought they to make their choice.

It is foolish to purport to have a definitive answer, but important to offer a plausible one, if only to focus attention on this vital area. Hence, I should like to suggest that we adopt the following as the principle of self-defence and defence of others:

> Every person is morally entitled and thereby is privileged to threaten or intentionally use force against another for the purpose of preventing or terminating what he reasonably believes to be a serious and unjust interference with his inalienable right or ability to fulfil basic human needs.

[10] Donnelly *et al.*, p. 663.

This principle, in essence, expresses the right of every person to just protection against undesirable death, injury, and ill health.

Lack of space prevents an extended discussion here, but it is not difficult to show that if this principle is carefully explicated, it also accounts for the various interpretations : for example, the secondary right to kill to protect property is based upon the notion that property and fundamental physico-chemical needs are mutually dependent; the secondary right to kill if necessary to prevent mental torture is based upon the need for self-respect and psychological security; and even the often-challenged right to kill to protect one's liberty depends, not merely upon a culturally determined sense of honour, but upon whether or not there is a basic human need to live and die with dignity.

IV

In this discussion, the following points have been stressed :

The most that can reasonably be expected of a moral theory of killing is that, aside from the usual cognitive desiderata, it be consistent with the basic principles of morality, and provide human beings with the clear and self-sufficient criteria which are necessary to make judgments both in paradigm-like and novel situations.

Moreover, since moral principles are essentially incomplete, it is preferable to express this principle in the form of a rule, the rule that, generally speaking, one ought not to kill a human being whose existence or actions neither have nor will cause imminent harm.

The moral principle of defence is best formulated when definitions by simple enumeration and opaque references, such as 'the right to defend against unlawful interferences', can be eliminated. The key question here is, what operational criteria ought be substituted? By way of reply, it has been suggested that a human being has a moral right to use force, if necessary deadly force, against another for the purpose of preventing or terminating what he reasonably believes to be a serious and unjust interference with his inalienable right or ability to fulfil basic needs.

PART II

Abortion

There are some things that all human beings have in common. One of these – perhaps the most important – is the capacity for suffering. We have it in our power to diminish immeasurably the sum of suffering and misery in the world, but we shall not succeed in this while we allow opposite irrational beliefs to divide the human race into mutually hostile groups. A wise humanity, in politics as elsewhere, comes only of remembering that even the largest groups are composed of individuals, that individuals can be happy or sad, and that every individual in the world who is suffering represents a failure of human wisdom and of common humanity.

Bertrand Russell, *Human Society in Ethics and Politics*

3

The Argument from Innocence

Of the many arguments against direct abortion,[1] there is one which makes an unusually strong prima facie case. It is the argument from innocence. 'Every living foetus,' we are told, 'regardless of its stage of development, is a human being and any act which is a deliberate and direct destruction of that innocent life is therefore an act of murder.'[2] Or more simply stated : the killing of an innocent human being is immoral. Abortion is the killing of an innocent human being. Therefore abortion is immoral.

Two questions must be answered. First, is it true that each and every killing of an innocent human being is immoral? And second, can we correctly say that a human foetus is a human being? I believe both questions are best answered in the negative and that the argument from innocence therefore must be rejected.

Law or Rule?

Consider the following situation. An obstetrician discovers in the middle of delivery that he is dealing with a twin pregnancy. It

---

[1] Theologians, especially Roman Catholics, distinguish direct from indirect abortion. They recognize 'direct abortion in which there is the direct intention to expel a non-viable, living foetus from the uterus; also indirect abortion in which the expulsion of the foetus is not directly procured, but occurs as a consequence of some other procedure'. John Marshall, *The Ethics of Medical Practice* (London: Darton, Longman & Todd, 1960), p. 103. I use 'abortion' hereafter to mean 'direct abortion'.

[2] Charles J. McFadden, op. cit., p. 135. Also Patrick Finney and Patrick O'Brien, *Moral Problems in Hospital Practice* (St Louis: B. Herder Co., 1956), p. 53.

is a case of locked twins; a case where the first child presents by the breech and the second by the vertex, where the two heads have locked in such a manner that the second fits into the neck of the first child making its delivery impossible. What should the physician do if he cannot displace the head of the second child? Should he decapitate the first and save the second? Or should he allow both to die?

Dissentient moralists, namely those who employ the argument from innocence, maintain that the proposed act of decapitation is a violation of the Fifth Commandment; 'Thou shalt not kill' is interpreted to mean 'Thou shalt not kill innocent human beings.' This command, we are told, is an expression of a universal, immutable, and absolute moral law. Regardless of the nobility or worthiness of the end or objective, man is never morally justified in taking an innocent human life. In the case of locked twins the physician should allow both to die.[3] For while it is definitely a sin *to kill* one innocent foetus, it is not a sin *to allow* both to die. The true choice, we are told, lies between the following : (i) directly killing an innocent human being and (ii) permitting (not causing) the death of both foetuses.

> The first, a moral evil, is immeasurably worse than the second, a merely physical evil. Hence, even considering the physician's action as a choice between two evils, it must be condemned. It is never permissible to commit a sin, a moral evil, in order to prevent any other evil, physical or moral. *It is preferable by far that a million mothers and foetuses perish than that a physician stain his soul with murder.*[4]

It would be an injustice to reply that all who believe and act in this manner are thoroughly heartless, though at times it seems as if this is the only conclusion that can be drawn. But we might well ask, why is it better that a million perish than that a physician kills an innocent human being? Does God really want

[3] John Marshall, op. cit., p. 121.
[4] Edwin F. Healy, op. cit., p. 196. The emphasis is my own.

it that way? If so, then can we in truth say that such a god is moral? If not, then what is the justification? What is it that proclaims that it is better that a million mothers and foetuses should perish than that a physician should endanger his immortal soul? Is it the voice of morality or the scintilla of self-interest?

I suspect that we are here faced not with a moral law but rather with a rule, a rule which if properly formulated would read: *generally speaking* one ought not to kill innocent human beings. The fact that it is a rule does not detract from its importance. Nor does it imply that exceptions are numerous. Nevertheless they do exist. For there are times when this rule conflicts with another moral rule, namely, that one ought to be as just as is humanly possible. In the case of the locked twins, justice requires that we make exception (I almost wrote take exception) to the rule concerning the killing of innocent human beings. For if it is unjust to kill one innocent human being, then it is a greater injustice to kill (or allow to die) two equally innocent human beings.

Thus far we have been assuming that a human foetus is a human being. If this is not the case then the major premise, in addition to being false, is irrelevant.

Is a Human Foetus a Human Being?

Various reasons are given in the hope of justifying an affirmative answer. Consider the argument, or at least one form of the argument, which appeals to the presence of the rational soul. Some writers conclude that, since Canon 747 of the Church states that a living aborted foetus, regardless of age, should be baptized unconditionally, this indicates that the Church deems a soul to be present from the moment of conception. Others follow St Thomas and claim that there is no human being at all during the first few weeks of pregnancy.[5] Now why should St Thomas be considered more of an authority than Church Law or vice

[5] J. Doncell, S.J., *Continuum*, Spring 1967, pp. 167–71.

versa? To answer by appealing to either authority is to beg the question.

A more convincing argument is one in which it is tacitly assumed that all classification is limited to the species-genus variety. Reasons are given to explain why a human foetus must be a member of *homo sapiens*. Then it is suggested that if a foetus belongs to the category *homo sapiens* it must be a human being. For example, St John-Stevas maintains that, since 'there is no qualitative difference between the embryo at the moment of conception and at the moment of quickening', the embryo must be considered a human being.[6] 'The stubborn fact,' writes Neuhaus, 'is that our contemporary understanding of the continuous process of life makes it difficult to exclude the prenatal child from the phenomenon of man.'[7] Apparently, *if a foetus is a member of the biological species homo sapiens it necessarily follows that that foetus is a human being.*

This problem is analogous to the problem of whether or not an acorn is an oak tree. If an acorn is destroyed, has a tree been killed? I think not. Something has been killed. Admittedly the living seed of an oak tree has been killed. But it is confusing to suggest that the killing of a seed of a tree is the same as killing a tree. The seed and the tree may both be members of the same growth form. But the seed is a member of the class of unborn progeny; the tree is not. Hence to say that a seed of an oak tree is an oak tree is to say (at least in part) that unborn progeny are born progeny.

Despite the obvious parallel between the 'seed-tree problem' and the 'human foetus – human being problem', there is one important difference. The latter gives rise to a mistake; the former does not. The question is, why?

Suppose two machines are constructed. The first has the ability of an ordinary, but not a fluent, speaker. The second has the ability of a fluent speaker, i.e., the second machine knows the

[6] Norman St John-Stevas, op. cit., p. 32.
[7] Richard John Neuhaus, 'The Dangerous Assumptions', *Commonweal*, Vol. 86, No. 15 (1967), p. 412.

language perfectly.[8] Each machine is given the task of distinguishing between contradictory and non-contradictory sentences and then fed the following sentences :

> (1) Every oak seed is an oak tree.
>
> (2) Every human foetus is a human being.

The first machine, the one with the ability of an ordinary but not a fluent speaker, rejects (1) for reasons that have already been mentioned. But it does not reject (2). Instead it adds the specification *being* to the term *human foetus* and concludes that by *every human foetus being* is meant that *every foetus which is a member of homo sapiens is a member of homo sapiens*. This machine fails as a fluent speaker to the extent that it fails to recognize the ambiguous use of *being* and the resulting contradictory sentence.

The second machine rejects both (1) and (2). There are several reasons for its rejection of (2). First, as a fluent speaker it understands that *being* is ambiguous in English : $being_1$ signifies that which has existence, while $being_2$ signifies an individual which has or has had an independent nature capable of sustaining and regulating its own metabolic pattern (in short, non-specific being and independent being). Second, it understands that the word *being* is being used ambiguously, that sentence (2) can be paraphrased to read *every human foetus $being_1$ is a human $being_2$*. Finally, and most important, it realizes that the underlying structure of this assertion is self-contradictory. The fluent English speaker understands that to assert that *every human foetus $being_1$ is a human $being_2$* is in essence to assert that *all unborn human progeny are born human progeny*.

Someone may object and say that this is merely an appeal to

[8] This is not to suggest that there is a fluent speaker or that such a machine could be constructed. The notion of a fluent speaker is an idealization in exactly the same sense which any scientific theory is. See: Noam Chomsky, *Aspects of the Theory of Syntax* (London and Cambridge, Mass. : M.I.T. Press, 1965), pp. 3–4. Jerrold J. Katz, *The Philosophy of Language*, op. cit., pp. 115–17.

English usage and that to discuss what silly people mean when they say silly things may be amusing but can hardly be important. This objection cannot be taken seriously. Life and death are not silly matters. Furthermore, no appeal has been made to what silly people mean. An appeal has been made to what is meant by *human being* in English. An appeal has been made to the structure of a language and not merely to its use. The difference is this : language is the depository of the accumulated body of experience to which all former ages have contributed their part. It contains a much deeper knowledge of the world than most of us suspect. Scrutiny of the structure of English reveals that all terms referring to living things convey either the idea of born or unborn progeny as part of their meaning. Just as *boy*, *bachelor* and *king* are words semantically characterized by the term *male*, the words *seed*, *egg*, and *foetus* are characterized by the term *unborn progeny*.

This is not to deny the phenomenon of language change. It is not to deny that certain sequences of sounds keep their meaning only by virtue of the tacit agreement of the general community of speakers. Nor is it to deny that a community can, under certain conditions, revoke its consent to the rules which are in force. *Bachelor*, which signifies 'a young man who has not married', has come to mean 'an unmarried person of marriageable age'. Therefore, it is no longer necessary to be a male in order to be correctly called a bachelor.

But there are good reasons for this particular change. First of all, it is offensive to call a young unmarried woman a spinster. Second, apart from the word *spinster* there is no other appropriate and partially synonymous term available. Third, although *bachelor* is (or is becoming) neutral, the important male-female distinction has not been lost; when the word is used to refer to individuals, the subject of the sentence usually indicates the gender : *She is a bachelor, Miss Jones is a bachelor*. But a similar case cannot be made for reducing the meaning of *human being* to that of *homo sapiens*. To give a term a meaning that another term in the language already has is needless duplication. Moreover, to discard 'born progeny' as part of the meaning of *human being* while keeping 'unborn progeny' as part of the meaning of *foetus* does not make sense. And the alternative, that of changing the meaning of *human being* and *foetus* (in effect discarding two good words), makes even less sense.

Let us, however, suppose that there is good reason for changing the meaning of *human being*. Let us assume that if abortion is immoral we are obligated to do whatever is necessary to the language in order to save lives. Now even if all this were true, we would still have to reject the argument from innocence. For it is not permissible to use a persuasive definition in order to guarantee the truth of a conclusion of an argument where the truth of the conclusion stands as the justification for the use of the persuasive definition. Or more simply put : it is not permissible to use a persuasive definition of *human being* in an argument which purports to prove that abortion is immoral and at the same time use the truth of this conclusion as the justification for the use of the persuasive definition. This procedure merely begs both questions.

4

The Slippery Slope

Consider the question of whether or not we can correctly say that a human foetus is a human being. I am inclined to believe that a negative answer is correct. Others disagree. They maintain that the foetus is a human being and usually advance some version of the 'slippery slope' argument in support of that claim.

The general form of the argument is that, since in the nature of things all change is discrete and continuous, lines or boundaries cannot be found, held, or adequately drawn. The version used in the abortion controversy says that the development of a human being from conception through birth into childhood is continuous and that to draw a line in this process is to make an arbitrary choice, a choice for which in the nature of things no good reason can be found or given. St John-Stevas and others maintain that, since there is no qualitative difference between the embryo at the moment of conception and at the moment of quickening, the embryo must be considered a human being.[1]

As I have suggested elsewhere,[2] this argument is fallacious. I thought, and still think, that it makes about as much sense to say that a foetus is a human being as it does to say that an acorn is an oak tree.

The analogy runs as follows: if an acorn is destroyed, has a

[1] Norman St John-Stevas, *The Right to Life*, op. cit., p. 32. For similar arguments, see: T. Goodrich, 'The Morality of Killing', *Philosophy*, April 1969, p. 137; John D. Dingell, *U.S. Congressional Record*, 91st Congress, 2nd Sess., 1970, Vol. 116, No. 182, pp. H10288–89.
[2] See pp. 42–43, and 'The Term "Human Being" and the Problem of Abortion', *Names*, September 1971, pp. 221–22.

tree been killed? I think not. Something has been killed. Admittedly the living seed of an oak tree has been killed. But it is mere confusion to suggest that the killing of a seed of a tree is the same as killing a tree. The seed and the tree may both be members of the same growth form. But the seed is a member of the class of unborn progeny; the tree is not. Hence to say that a seed of an oak tree is an oak tree is to say (at least in part) that unborn progeny are born progeny.

An explanation was also advanced as to why speakers rarely make mistakes when talking about acorns and oak trees, but err when talking about more exalted matters. The assumption being made, which I regard as mistaken, is that the meaning of a compound noun is always the result of a single combination of non-ambiguous components and that this combination never involves a shift in meaning. I suggested that the word *being* is ambiguous : *being*$_1$ signifies 'that which has existence', while *being*$_2$ signifies 'an individual that has or has had an independent nature capable of sustaining and regulating its own metabolic pattern' (in short, non-specific being and independent being). A fluent speaker, I went on to argue, would not say that every human foetus (being$_1$) is a human being$_2$ because he understands that in essence this is to assert that all unborn human progeny are born human progeny, and that this is self-contradictory. I continue to think it is enlightening to compare a foetus to an acorn, that it is self-contradictory to assert that every human foetus (being$_1$) is a human being$_2$, and that the lines drawn in the language reflect important distinctions. Not only are there objective differences, but I seriously doubt whether a pregnant woman or a mother would view the distinction between unborn and born progeny to be as arbitrary and unimportant as our 'slippery slope'-minded colleagues would have us believe. However, there is a point upon which I was mistaken. It was a mistake to believe that such fallacies occur simply because of semantic oversight or confusion.

Lines can be, and are, reasonably drawn, especially in the case of material objects and related processes. Better yet, and a stronger claim for the fluent speaker,[3] all material-object and related-process words denote perfectly determinate classes. When deciding whether or not something is to be named by linguistic items of this kind, the fluent speaker is never troubled by border-line cases. He, for example, has no difficulty in distinguishing water from ice, acorns from oak trees, and foetuses from born progeny.

Whether or not certain levels of language are perfectly deter-minate is not important; at least not in this context. What is important is that advocates of the 'slippery slope' should be taking the opposite tack. If they were consistent they would argue that all material-object and related-process words are indeterminate or vague. But they do not. They do not, and I suspect would not, want to argue that we cannot reasonably distinguish red from orange, milk from cheese, and acorns from oak trees. But if this is the case, why should the 'slippery slope' be used in the abortion debate? Why, so to speak, 'pick on' the term 'human being'?

We need not look far for an answer. Bart Heffernan, in his Amicus Curiae Brief,[4] provides part of the explanation when he says that 'Human life is a continuum, and if those at one end can be exterminated, why not those at the other?'[5] Or, as a colleague has asked : once you draw new lines, once you say it is permissible to kill human foetuses (that is, to kill less than fully potential human beings), then how does one limit the killing to that of foetuses? How does one hold the line and prevent the killing of the mentally retarded, the handicapped, the elderly, or members of any group who have not achieved, or have lost, their full potential as human beings?

As might be expected, we have an answer to our question, but the answer is less credulous than the original argument. Why is it that adequate lines can be drawn between permissible and non-

---

[3] A *fluent speaker* is 'one who has perfect linguistic competence and whose performance matches that competence'.

[4] Brief and Appendices of Dr Bart Heffernan, Amicus Curiae in Support of Appellant. *United States of America vs. Milan Vuitch*, Supreme Court of the United States, October 1970, No. 84, pp. 1–45.

[5] Ibid., p. 26.

permissible killing, but cannot be drawn between born and unborn progeny? Is the line between permissible killing and non-permissible killing more natural than the line between the unborn and the born? Is human life more of a continuum than a series of graded acts of killing? Moreover, why can't we hold the newly proposed line? If we can kill in self-defence, in capital punishment, and in wartime, if these exceptions can be made, then why can't abortion be another exception? Why is the line between a combatant and non-combatant in wartime (to choose just one example) easier to hold than the line between killing human foetuses and killing human beings?

The basic issue here is whether or not the idea of killing is contagious. That is, whether or not a person, group, or society – exposed to actual killing or the idea of sanctioned killing – universalizes and thereby extends this domain. I think this question is best answered in the negative : there is overwhelming evidence that human beings compartmentalize their ideas, and it is only when the normal process of compartmentalization breaks down that one encounters difficulties.[6]

This doesn't mean that human beings don't make mistakes. But it does mean that in the normal process of generalization there are constraints. And one of the more important constraints is that the process is limited by the concept of 'same kind or same class of objects'. For example, if we crush an insect and believe this to be a permissible act, we do not conclude that it is permissible to kill all living things. We only conclude that it is permissible to kill that kind of insect, or at most, all kinds of insects. Similarly, if we are taught to kill Nazis and the criteria for a Nazi and the circumstances of permissible killings are clearly spelled out, we do not kill all German nationals (although of the possible mistakes this is probably the most likely). We do not mistakenly generalize and kill all Europeans. Nor do we proceed, either in fact or in mind, to kill all human beings.

Of course it would be absurd to deny that the ability to draw

[6] For a treatment of this and related issues, see the section on consequentialist arguments, pp. 14–20.

and hold conceptual lines is a function of intelligence. But the level of intelligence required is not high, and the man of average intelligence easily makes these distinctions and judgments. I say this because it is important to strike out against the view which maintains that new or heterodox views of morals ought not to be considered or taught, because the masses are unintelligent. Although this is a favourite elitist tactic, it is, nonetheless, pernicious nonsense.

5

Women's Liberation and the Argument for Abortion on Request

> Modern feminists are no longer so anxious as the
> feminists of thirty years ago to curtail the 'vices' of
> men; they ask rather that what is permitted to men
> shall be permitted also to them. Their predecessors
> sought equality in moral slavery, whereas they seek
> equality in moral freedom.

> Bertrand Russell,
> *Marriage and Morals*
> (1929)

Spokeswomen for the women's movement maintain that all
women have the moral and legal right to control their own repro-
ductive lives. Legally, this entails the removal from penal codes of
laws limiting access to contraceptive information and devices, and
all laws governing abortion.[1] Morally, it means that a foetus may
be destroyed upon request any time before its birth. Indeed, 'one
of the few things everyone in the women's movement seems to
agree on is that we have to get rid of the abortion laws and
make sure that any woman who wants an abortion can get one'.[2]
It is true that there is some difference of opinion concerning the
issue of viability and the political significance of the abortion
issue. Nonetheless, 'all feminists would agree that it is a woman's
basic and inalienable right to limit her reproduction'.[3]

[1] 1968 National Organization for Women Bill of Rights, Section VIII.
[2] Lucinda Cisler, 'Abortion Law Repeal (Sort of): A Warning to Women',
in *Women's Liberation,* compiled by Sookie Stambler (New York: Ace
Books, 1970), p. 72.
[3] Judith Hule and Ellen Levine, *Rebirth of Feminism* (New York: Quad-
rangle Books, 1971), p. 302.

My strategy is a simple one. I shall defend the moderate feminist position.[4] I shall not aim at refutation, although in some cases the counter-argument will amount to such. Instead I will be content to show that the most powerful criticisms of the moderate (hereafter referred to simply as the feminist) position fail to hit their mark. These criticisms are :

I   That foeticide is contagious, and that the destruction of unborn lives must, sooner or later, lead to universal misfortune;

II   That contrary to feminist claims, compulsory pregnancy neither destroys nor infringes upon a woman's dignity;

III   That each unborn human infant is a human being is a fact beyond dispute; and

IV   That the human foetus has a natural and inalienable right to life, and, since it is an innocent being, its destruction is murder.

Not all opponents of abortion use these arguments. Nor are they of equal weight. But taken together they make an impressive initial case against abortion, and therefore ought to be understood and carefully replied to.

I

Many opponents of abortion believe that foeticide is contagious. In their minds, abortion must become, or actually is, the cause of greater non-foetal homicide. This view is, of course, in every

[4] Both the radical and moderate feminist favour abortion upon request. But the radical feminist maintains that, since the foetus is always merely *pars viscerum matris*, like an appendix, it has no prima facie moral right to life. The moderate feminist, on the other hand, maintains that a living potential human being has the prima facie right to life, but that the actual right may be reasonably denied in cases of abortion on request. The difference is not as insignificant as it may seem. For the denial of the prima facie right to life is tantamount to a denial of all rights, and often of all moral and legal protection.

way inadequate. For example, according to the Federal Bureau of Investigation, the murder and non-negligent manslaughter rate in the United States increased from 4·5 in 1962 to 7·8 in 1970. The homicide rate therefore was rising long before the few liberalized abortion laws went into effect. So that if one wants to argue that the new abortion laws were the initial causal factors, one would have to make a case for the causal efficacy of future events, that is, make a case for reverse causation.

Should this be modified and the lesser claim made that the new laws were only contributory factors, there still remains a problem of justification. For the evidence does not substantiate this charge, and the opponents of abortion, with all their eloquence, have not presented a convincing empirical case. If foeticide were truly contagious why would there be an increase in the murder and non-negligent manslaughter rates of groups other than the classes of aborted mothers and responsible physicians? Is this not like saying disease X is contagious, but only for those who have neither direct nor indirect contact with those who have X?

But if our argument is sound, then why do so many thinkers persist in believing that foeticide is contagious?

Two related conjectures might be advanced. The first is that the moral or legal sanction of abortion is believed to be a dangerous reversal of the powerful historical trend to reduce all forms of killing. The fear is that, if we do not protect the foetus, we should be abandoning the forces of history and withdrawing our protection from all beings who never have been able to, or no longer can, measure up as fully developed, morally free, human agents. Legalizing abortion is in effect to sign the death warrant for unwanted animals, infants, the mentally retarded or mentally ill, comatose patients and the elderly.

The second is that we are dealing with a theory that is not only held *a priori*, but apparently cannot be faulted by evidence. It is the venerable theory that innately man has both the desire to kill and the disposition to enjoy the death of others. This point of view was given perhaps its most brilliant expression by Freud.

According to Freud, primitive man was 'a very violent being, more cruel and more malign than other animals. He liked to kill, and killed as a matter of course'.[5]

> The first and most portentous prohibition of the awakening of the conscience was: Thou shalt not kill. It was born of the reaction against that hate-gratification which lurked behind the grief for the loved dead, and was gradually extended to unloved strangers and finally even to enemies. . . . So powerful a prohibition can only be directed against an equally powerful impulse. What no human soul desires there is no need to prohibit; it is automatically excluded. The very emphasis of the commandment, *Thou shalt not kill*, makes it certain that we spring from an endless ancestry of murders, with whom the lust for killing was in the blood, as possibly it is to this very day with ourselves.[6]

We should take care not to jump to the conclusion that this logically entails an opposition to abortion or that opponents of abortion hold a theory with all the Freudian nuances. What seems to be generally held is the belief that within each human breast beats the heart of a potentially murderous brute, a brute that will surely be awakened and released once abortion is morally or legally sanctioned.

To these ingenious appeals, I reply: (i) Historically, there has been little opposition to killing *per se*. There has been some but not overwhelming opposition to unjust killing and a still stronger movement against cruel killing. Perhaps the most powerful opposition has been to cruel and unjust killing. (ii) To confuse cruel and/or unjust killing with killing *per se* is to muddle the basic moral issue. (iii) It remains to be shown that legalized abortion is by its very nature cruel or unjust. And if it is not, the moral dangers of a slide are more fiction than fact. (iv) The evidence we have of primitive man indicates that he was neither

---

[5] Sigmund Freud, 'Thoughts for the Times on War and Death' (1915), *Collected Papers* (London: Hogarth Press, 1925), Vol. IV, p. 308.
[6] Ibid., pp. 311–312.

more nor less violent than we are. (v) The existence of a powerful moral prohibition does not in itself show that it is directed against an equally powerful impulse. That we, for example, have a powerful taboo against sodomy does not mean that man has an equal impulse or instinct for this form of canalization. (vi) 'Aggression, far from being the diabolical, destructive principle that classical psychoanalysis makes it out to be, is really an essential part of the life-preserving organization of instincts.'[7] (vii) If we are taught with a reasonable degree of care what are the defining characteristics of members of the class it is permissible to kill, then this is an adequate safeguard, and (aside from accident) in no way entails killing others. (viii) In the case of abortion a line is, and can continue to be safely, drawn between unborn and born progeny, and therefore foeticide does not entail or threaten the killing of other members of society.

II

What is felt when a woman faced with compulsory pregnancy senses a loss of dignity?

Feminist literature is abundantly clear as to the sort of loss felt. Radical feminists maintain that the popularized version of love has 'been used politically to cloud and justify an oppressive relationship between men and women, and that in reality there can be no genuine love until the need to *control* the growth of another is substituted by the love *for* the growth of another'.[8] 'Most of us recognize,' writes Cisler, 'that "reforms" of the old rape-incest-foetal-deformity variety are not in women's interest and in fact, in their very specificity are almost more an insult to our dignity as active, self-determining humans than are the old laws that simply forbid us to have abortion unless we are about to die.'[9] And Kate Millett expresses the felt brutality when she says that indirectly one form of 'death penalty' still obtains in

[7] Konrad Lorenz, *On Aggression* (London: Methuen, 1966; Toronto: Bantam Books, 1963), p. 44.
[8] *A Manifesto for New York Radical Feminists*, 1969.
[9] Cisler, op. cit., p. 75.

America today, since 'patriarchal legal systems in depriving women of control over their own bodies drive them to illegal abortions. . . .'[10]

We are being told two things : first, that compulsory pregnancy offers a choice between a form of slavery and possible death; and second, that what shatters the sense of dignity is not the knowledge that the women in question must suffer, but that they must suffer *needlessly* because of society's lack of respect for their rights.

I shall not dwell on the reply that, because dignity is an intrinsic part of being human, it cannot be destroyed by compulsory pregnancy. This may raise interesting theoretical questions but is beside the point. For not only are feminists not claiming a loss of intrinsic dignity, it would be patently absurd for them to do so. The reason is that if 'human dignity is the kind of intrinsic worth which attaches to a human being in his capacity of being a responsible person',[11] and if we cannot destroy this inner worth and claim, then it follows that we cannot destroy the dignity of a living human being, and it makes little sense to discuss that possibility.

Yet at least two things are amiss. First of all, to tell a woman who is oppressed and suffering that she has intrinsic dignity is like consoling a concentration camp prisoner by telling him that he is metaphysically free. Second, there is the injustice of having a double standard. For the anti-abortionist maintains that no amount of sexism or compulsory pregnancy can effect a woman's true worth, and, on the other hand, claims that having an abortion shatters a human being's sense of dignity because it is a horrible, squalid and brutal action. Surely he cannot have it both ways.

Dignity, as a moral quality or characteristic of a human being, is a comparatively difficult notion to grasp. But I think both parties to the dispute would agree that dignity is closely related

---

[10] Kate Millet, *Sexual Politics* (London: Hart-Davis, 1971; New York: Doubleday, 1970), pp. 43–4.

[11] Herbert Spiegelberg, 'Human Dignity: A Challenge', *The Philosophy Forum*, Vol. 9, Nos. 1 & 2 (1971), p. 60.

in nature to respect, that there is at least one sense of the term in which we say that the having of dignity requires respectful treatment; or, perhaps more accurately, that the losing of dignity requires disrespectful treatment. Care, of course, should be taken not to confuse respect-for-an-ability with respect-for-a-person as a human being. I may not respect Mary or John's plumbing ability, but nonetheless may respect each as a person. On the other hand, if I fail to respect a mature person's ability to freely function in major areas of human endeavour such as work or sex (assuming they have the capacity to so function), then to that degree, I fail to respect them as persons.

The feminist charge, as I understand it, is twofold. First, it is that as a class of human beings women are treated disrespectfully. For women do not have equal opportunity to select their vocation, to obtain work, to advance on the basis of merit, and so forth. Moreover, sexual freedom is denied in the name of virginity (or the equally extreme cult of non-virginity, i.e., the having of sex upon male demand), and the double standard. It is also denied by making contraception physically or psychologically unavailable, and by forcing women to bear unwanted children. Thus :

> by legally forbidding a prospective mother to have an abortion she wants, the state causes her misery and restricts her freedom to act in what she believes to be her own best interest. To force her to continue her pregnancy and to bear a child she does not want is to work a certain violence upon her. It is to refuse to respect her integrity as a human being. And doing this is the more grotesque because the state thereby ignores her intrinsic worth as a human being while pretending to guarantee the intrinsic worth of a merely potential human being.[12]

Second, that since the lack of respect is endemic and a powerful anti-woman bias exists, it is extremely difficult for many men to

[12] Robert Hoffman, 'The Moral Right to Abortion', *Michigan Quarterly Review*, Vol. 8, No. 4 (1969), p. 277.

objectively understand or discuss the problem of abortion. Both charges, I think, are valid. Yet, the second may be misunderstood. I am not saying, as militant feminists often do, that only women can understand the problem of abortion, a contention that is straightforwardly false. Nor am I saying that all opposition to abortion is the result of sexism. To fight for a better way of life is not necessarily sexist. To demand that we do not act rashly or carelessly in important matters, or that no one should harm another unless provoked by an injury, is often to demand that we act morally and nothing more. Yet the charge of bias is an interesting one. For when we turn to the question of the morality of killing the foetus, the opponent of abortion cannot successfully escape from the charge that society's sexist attitudes do prejudice the discussion of what it means to be a human being or to be morally innocent.

III

Before we examine the question of the unwanted foetus's moral entitlement, it will be well to consider how far we may reasonably go in determining whether or not a human foetus is a human being.

It certainly seems natural, and the aim of most of the literature has been, to identify a characteristically human essence or function, and then proceed to argue that the foetus either has or has not the said characteristic. The presupposition is that, although the question may be a difficult one, it is capable of objective solution. And by 'objective solution' is meant that the sentence 'a human foetus is a human being' often expresses a proposition, and when it does it has truth-value. At the other end of the philosophical spectrum we find the opposite claim, and one that is presented most ably by Roger Wertheimer.[13] According to Wertheimer, we seem to be struck with the indeterminateness of the foetus's humanity.

[13] Roger Wertheimer, 'Understanding the Abortion Argument', *Philosophy & Public Affairs*, Vol. 1, No. 1 (1971), pp. 67–95.

This does not mean that, whatever you believe, it is true or true for you if you believe it. Quite the contrary, it means that, whatever you believe, it's not true – but neither is it false. You believe it, and that's the end of the matter.[14]

I do not wish to undervalue Wertheimer's general contribution which represents both excellence in understanding and a fair-mindedness seldom found in the literature. I think, however, that when we consider his premises concerning the status of the foetus, they must be admitted to be open to certain objections.

In the first place, we do not seem to be struck with the indeterminateness of the foetus's humanity, if by 'we' is meant the majority. For the majority clearly holds that if Y's parents are of X growth-form, then Y is an X. So that if a foetus is procreated by human parents, then aside from the vagaries of genetic change, it is human, at least in the biological sense of that term.

The difficulty here is not that Wertheimer would deny this, but rather that his use of language is loose enough to warrant this interpretation. For by emulating the looseness of ordinary usage, by using the expressions 'a human', 'a human being', 'a person', as 'virtually interchangeable', he accurately reproduces the obscurity, and possible confusion, that besets ordinary language.

What makes this more curious is that Wertheimer believes our understanding of the abortion argument is greatly facilitated by distinguishing between the extreme liberal, liberal, moderate, conservative and extreme conservative positions. But the relationship between these terms and their references are not in the nature of things. Wertheimer does not – nor does anyone else – have a rule of life from which it follows that when an individual argues that such and such is true of abortion, then he or she must either be a liberal, moderate or conservative. Yet once we adequately settle upon or stipulate meanings for these terms (as Wertheimer does), we admittedly contribute to the understanding of the problem of abortion. Why not then do the same for the term

[14] Ibid., pp. 88–9.

'human' and its cognates? Why not distinguish between different senses of 'a human life', 'a human being', 'person', so that while some may be fully synonymous at least one string would not?

Note that this move does not beg the question. For its purpose is not that of settling the disagreement but of providing a method by which we can more easily understand exactly what is being controverted.

I suspect that Wertheimer would accept at least part of this strategy, but be inclined to reject the idea that these words have different senses, or its correlate, namely, that they are ambiguous. For he maintains first, that an illocution presupposes 'the performance of an act of using a particular pheme (sentence) with a certain more or less definite sense and a more or less definite reference' and that therefore an illocution cannot be ambiguous;[15] second, that 'a sentence is ambiguous if and only if its utterance on some occasion is reasonably construable as being either of two (or more) illocutions which differ not merely (if at all) in being two different kinds of illocutions'.[16] Applying this to the problem of abortion, we obtain the following: Since an illocution is by definition an expression that is used with a certain more or less definite sense and a more or less definite reference, and is therefore not ambiguous, and since almost all utterances which contain the expression 'human' or its cognates are so used, it follows therefore that almost all of them are not ambiguous.

I shall not dwell on the dubious notions of having 'a more or less definite sense' or 'a more or less definite reference'. Instead I shall be content to suggest, first, that this is not so much a theory of ambiguity as a theory as to its relative insignificance, and second, that so conceived, the theory only serves to obscure the problem of multiple meaning. For example, suppose a feminist says S₁, that 'a human foetus is not necessarily a human being' meaning that 'a foetus which has the genetic attributes of *homo sapiens* is not necessarily an individual which has or has had an

[15] Roger Wertheimer, *The Significance of Sense* (Ithaca and London: Cornell University Press, 1972), p. 68.
[16] Ibid., p. 72.

independent nature capable of sustaining and regulating its own metabolic pattern'. Suppose the conservative counters by saying S_2, that 'a human foetus is necessarily a human being', meaning that 'a foetus which has the genetic attributes of *homo sapiens* is necessarily a member of that growth-form'. Now one can say, as I imagine Wertheimer would, that S_1 and S_2 are not ambiguous, and that what was unclear was what illocutions were being produced. But whatever one wants to call this phenomenon (i) it depends upon the existence of multiple word senses; (ii) the senses used in the above utterances are semantically non-deviant, which suggests the existence of constraints other than the speaker's intentions; (iii) by explicating the two senses of 'human' and paraphrasing S_1 and S_2 it becomes clearer to us what is meant; (iv) and most important, S_1 and S_2 express different but nonetheless true propositions.

So that even if we had no doubts about the merits of his theory of ambiguity, we should still be perplexed by Wertheimer's conclusion that 'it is not true that the foetus is a human being, but it is not false either' and therefore that 'the assertion that the foetus is a human being cannot be assigned a genuine truth-value'.[17] For if some utterances are not optative illocutions, then they can be assigned a genuine truth-value. And if this is the case, then greater care should be taken to distinguish between a speaker's values and interests in choosing a definition, and the meaning of the definition he actually chooses to use. That the choice of definition may be one of personal preference is true. But that the definition must be of an optative nature is not. And when it is not, then the assertion 'the foetus is a human being' is either true or false. Or more cautiously : when the sentence is neither deviant nor optative, then it is either true or false.

Given this analysis, the feminist charge of bias takes on a new and more sinister aspect. For if the definitions of 'human being' advanced in discussions about the morality of abortion were all rhetorical, persuasive, or internally morally loaded, then we would be tempted to dismiss them en masse. We would be able

[17] Wertheimer, 'Understanding the Abortion Argument', op. cit., p. 86.

to say that it is all propaganda or its like. That since there is a powerful sexist bias against women, most of the propaganda is anti-abortion, and ought therefore to be dismissed. But we should not go by this route, and it is important to understand why not.

Part of the answer has already been provided; namely, that some illocutions have truth-value. But the better part of the answer lies elsewhere, and constitutes what perhaps might be called political strategy.

Students of propaganda know that the best propaganda technique is often one that uses truth, provided of course the truth is highly credible. We also know that one of the worst mistakes to be made in countering this sort of attack is to disregard or to attempt to fault the truth. Now when it comes down to obtaining the best counter-strategy, much depends upon the situation. Nonetheless, the general rule is to belittle the importance of the particular item of truth by showing it to be indecisive or irrelevant.

This means that to argue, as many do, that no anti-abortion assertion about the foetus can be true is simply self-defeating. For example, when the anti-abortionist claims that 'each unborn human infant is a human being is *a fact* beyond dispute', meaning only that each infant is a member of *homo sapiens*, what he says is a fact, and one we ought not dispute. Two things ought to be done. We should remind the anti-abortionist, first, that while he may choose a sense of 'human being' which defines a foetus as either in or out of humanity, there is no adequate way of showing that the foetus already possesses characteristics entitling it to the equal rights of human beings; and second, that when compulsive pregnancy is the cause of actual misery, or the misery a prospective mother is virtually certain to feel, the innocence of the foetus is *not* beyond question.

IV

In the opening section of this chapter, I was careful to point out that those who morally favour abortion upon request are either saying that a living potential human being has no prima facie moral right to life or that, while it has this prima facie right, the actual right may reasonably be denied in certain circumstances. It is necessary, therefore, in order to complete our examination, to consider whether the unborn correctly can be said to have rights, and if so, to what extent the actual right to life may be justifiably denied.

To avoid confusion, it should be observed that the term 'right' is commonly used in two ways. It is sometimes applied to a sort of claim, power, or entitlement which is, or ought to be recognized because it rests upon specific legal sanctions, or more broadly upon such documents as The United States Constitution, The European Convention for the Protection of Human Rights and Fundamental Freedoms, The United Nations Declaration of Human Rights, and so forth. It is also applied to those sorts of entitlements which, irrespective of their recognition by any political body or document, human beings are said to have. Although the two areas of reference may overlap, they need not. Moreover, even if, according to some legal document or its like, it were decided that the foetus did not have an actual right to life in certain stages of its development or circumstances, legal decisions are not necessarily sound moral ones.

Moral thinkers differ widely in their opinions as to the grounds and nature of moral rights. Some maintain that rights are in themselves first-order moral principles; others, that rights are to be systematically deduced from principles like that of justice, beneficence, and so forth. I propose to follow the latter view. In this section, then, I shall use the term 'right' to denote those general entitlements which, though open to direct intuition, more adequately should be said to follow from the two basic principles of morality, that of justice and need utility. The former tells us that we should avoid treating differently, or discriminating between, individuals whose cases are similar in all important respects, that the just society makes the same proportionate contribution to the welfare of each citizen, in an effort to make all as nearly equally well off as possible; the latter that we ought

to minimize human misery and those conditions which interfere
with the satisfaction of basic needs.

The first point to notice in considering the question of who
has rights is that the obvious answer – free moral agents – seems
to eliminate the foetus as a possible direct recipient. For the
foetus, especially in its early stages of development can pass
neither the test of freedom nor that of rationality. Moreover, given
that only free moral agents may possess rights, there seems to be
no way of showing adequately that the foetus already possesses
characteristics entitling it to rights *equal* to those of free moral
agents.

One may be tempted to say that we should talk and act *as if*
higher animals and those born of human parents possessed
rights. So that at least some animals, human foetuses, infants,
the mentally afflicted and incurable lunatics may be thereby
protected. I am much in sympathy with this approach. But I
think it better to avoid the ways of moral fictionalism and to say
simply that we are *extending unequal rights*, and that in order
to be a recipient one does not have to be a free moral agent.

The obvious question, then, is why extend rights; why not
have none at all? The usual answer – that by forbidding the
cruel treatment of any sensitive being we increase feelings of
benevolence and therefore increase the common good – is not
well founded. For one thing, it is not at all clear that by forbidding cruel acts one effectively increases feelings of benevolence.
Nor does it follow that the having of such feelings necessarily
results in beneficence, although it surely disposes one to act kindly.
Fortunately, there are other reasons which weigh the scales heavily
in favour of extending rights, including the right not to be
treated cruelly. First of all, prudence favours the extension as a
form of moral insurance, since it knows that we or our loved
ones may be struck down by catastrophic illness or accident. Yet,
it is more than a question of prudence. The good or welfare of
sensitive beings have to a degree become affiliated closely with,
and often part of, the free moral agent's own good or welfare.
So that the grounds for protecting these beings become clear.

Extended rights ought to be claimed by free moral agents on behalf of those sensitive beings, the complete violation or disregarding of whose interests would result in misery or seriously interfere with the satisfaction of the basic needs of free moral agents.

Granting then that we should extend rights, and that these rights will be less than those of free moral agents, the question is how much less?

On one or two points we seem to be in general agreement; e.g., that no sensitive being ought to be killed cruelly; and perhaps that we have special duties to children as well as to those higher animals or other sensitive beings who have served us well. But beyond a few statements of this kind, it is very difficult to proceed. For example, in the case of higher animals we say that they can rightfully be killed, but not tormented or killed cruelly. Indeed, a man who torments a dog or horse is often considered more villainous than the person who torments his peers. Or again, hunters consider it an obligation to track down and kill a wounded animal.

Again, we may notice that in research involving animal subjects it is permissible to use substances or devices which can lead to the production of severe toxic effects or even death. This, however, is not permissible in experimentation involving humans.

What seems to follow from this is (i) that cruelty should always be avoided; and (ii) that one should always have a sound reason for the killing of higher animals, which usually comes down to meaning that these acts are justifiable only if they prevent the harming of, or bring benefit to mankind or its individual members. What is true of higher animals seems to me still more manifestly true of the viable foetus.[18] Cruelty should be avoided and one should always have sound reason for killing. Concerning the latter, it seems necessary at least to maintain that the killing

---

[18] It is considerably more difficult to determine the non-viable foetus's extended rights, which presumably it has. For while one may be inclined to believe that the foetus in any stage of its development is entitled to the same right to life as any higher animal, it is difficult to understand why a fertilized egg is so entitled. Of course, cruelty should be avoided, but beyond that I see no easy answer.

of a viable foetus is justifiable only if it prevents the harming[19] of at least its mother. So that among other things the viable foetus is protected and prevented from becoming a possible source of food, an object of commercial exploitation, or the new humanoid guinea pig. Viability is the compelling point because the foetus is then a being which has an independent nature capable of sustaining and regulating its own metabolic pattern.

Before concluding I wish briefly to consider and reply to two standard objections. The first is that the foetus is morally innocent and that therefore its killing is murder. Feminists and other advocates of abortion tend not to take this charge seriously; for they believe it rests solely upon the principle that one ought never to kill an innocent human being, and that therefore it is sufficient to deny that the foetus is a human being. In this they are mistaken. For it is also held that it is wrong to kill an innocent potential human being, a claim that I now wish to examine.

We say that X is

innocent$_1$ if X is not guilty of violating certain rules or laws;

innocent$_2$ if X's existence or actions neither have nor will cause imminent harm;

innocent$_3$ if X neither deliberately intends (intended to), nor actually has caused harm.

Other variations are possible, but these account for the major intended meanings of the sanctity-of-life principle.

I have suggested elsewhere[20] that innocent$_1$ is almost vacuous. Suffice it to say here that, unless the underlying moral rules or laws are explicated, we have no intelligent way of evaluating the claim that 'a potential human being is always innocent$_1$'. To say that 'a potential human being is always innocent$_2$' is simply false;

[19] 'Harm' is defined, for our purposes, as the violation of an interest or need, where interests and needs are carefully distinguished from mere desire or want.
[20] See pp. 29–30.

for some foetuses will cause harm. To say that 'a potential human being is innocent₃' is problematic; for the sentence seems to be semantically deviant. Suppose someone said 'the circle is innocent₃' or 'the green tie is innocent₃'. Would we want to say that these statements are necessarily true? Or would we try to show that only beings *who are capable of deliberately intending* are capable of being innocent₈? Of the two alternatives, the latter is obviously less misleading. Therefore, unless the opponent of abortion is using still another sense of the term, to say that a potential human foetus is always innocent is to either make a false or semantically deviant claim.

The second objection is that nothing has been said here or established elsewhere that prevents a woman from having an abortion for no reason at all. Now, by way of reply, it is of course true that such a preventative has neither been formulated nor, to my knowledge, been established. But even if we assume that it would be possible to do so, it by no means follows that there are good grounds for believing that a significant number of women would have an abortion for no reason at all. Again, I know of no empirical ground for supposing that a woman would frivolously kill her own child. Why then, in spite of the evidence, is this supposition widely held? My conjecture is that the feminists are right. That we have come full circle, that we have uncovered the most deadly anti-women bias of them all, namely : that unless women are carefully controlled they will kill their own progeny without reason because they are not fully rational creatures. What is there to say? Except that of all forms of wrongdoing few are viler than that of the pseudo-paternalist who, when he is most irrational, sees fit to deny the rationality of other human beings.

PART III

Euthanasia

I see there is an instinctive horror of killing living beings under any circumstances whatever. For instance, an alternative has been suggested in the shape of confining even rabid dogs in a certain place and allowing them to die a slow death. Now my idea of compassion makes this thing impossible for me. I cannot for a moment bear to see a dog, or for that matter any other living being, helplessly suffering the torture of a slow death. I do not kill a human being thus circumstanced because I have more hopeful remedies. I should kill a dog similarly situated because in its case I am without a remedy. Should my child be attacked with rabies and there was no helpful remedy to relieve his agony, I should consider it my duty to take his life.

Mahatma Gandhi,
Young India,
November 18, 1926

6

The Word 'Mercy' and the Problem of Kind Killing

Advocates of voluntary euthanasia are committed to the view that in certain circumstances and with specific safeguards the taking of human life is merciful. Opponents, on the other hand, argue that an act of euthanasia is not an act of mercy and therefore should not be performed. Both parties to this dispute seem to agree that if an act is merciful it is morally justified, but they disagree about euthanasia being merciful.

To clarify the nature of this disagreement it is necessary to ask and answer two questions. They are:

1. What, in this controversy, is meant by the word 'mercy'?

2. Is the proposition 'Some acts of euthanasia are merciful' true or false?

I shall maintain, first, that in this dispute the word 'mercy' has been used equivocally, and second, that because of this equivocation we have at least two different propositions to consider, one of which is true, the other false. I believe that the advocates and opponents of euthanasia are disputing two different points, and, that given the sense in which advocates of euthanasia use the word 'mercy', it is true to say that 'Some acts of euthanasia are merciful'.

Consider the following situation. Two fluent speakers in English – X and Y – appraise a case of euthanasia in which it is true (i) that the patient had excruciating pain; (ii) that the patient had to die as a result of the conditions causing the pain;

71

(iii) that the patient (an adult) did voluntarily favour some means of 'easy death'; (iv) that the death was painless; and (v) that the physician was motivated solely by the desire to satisfy the patient's request for an 'easy death'. X and Y agree about the facts of this case. But they disagree about whether or not the doctor's act was merciful.

Puzzled by this apparent disagreement X and Y decide to paraphrase their remarks. That is, they decide to substitute other words for the word 'mercy' without changing the original meaning of their respective statements.

Instead of X saying,

(1A) 'That was an act of mercy,'

he now says,

(1B) 'That was the kindest possible treatment of an unfortunate individual.'

Instead of Y saying,

(2A) 'That was not an act of mercy,'

he now says,

(2B) 'That was not an act of compassion and forbearance.'

This manœuvre exposes the source of the misunderstanding. The word 'mercy' being an abstract term is, more often than not, equivocated on when people argue that euthanasia is or is not merciful. Advocates of euthanasia tend to identify acts as being merciful only if they result in the kindest possible treatment of unfortunate individuals. Opponents tend to identify acts as being merciful if they result in compassionate and forbearing treatment. I think it is obvious that when this is true the alleged disputants are making different but not contradictory assertions.

Of course this does not in any way imply that there are two and only two legitimate senses of the word 'mercy'. Other equivocations are possible but they are not as common. Nor does it imply that every disagreement can be reduced to a purely verbal disagreement; for this simply is not true. What I am suggesting is that in many of these cases the disputants are not really at odds with each other.

Two objections usually arise at this point. One involves the notion that the word 'mercy' has one and only one correct meaning. 'Granted,' the critic would say, 'that the word "mercy" is often used equivocally. But it is one thing to say a word has been used in two different senses and still another to say that a word has been used in two equally good senses. Or, to put the matter somewhat differently, it is a mistake to suggest that both speakers have been equally duped by the language. The only one who has been duped is the speaker who points to a physician's act and says, "That is an act of mercy". After all, a patient is not guilty of a crime. What has he done that we must forgive? What impending punishment must we dispense with? What act of retribution must we abstain from? There simply is none. For a patient is innocent. Therefore it is a mistake to refer to an act, an act which involves an innocent patient, and say that "That is an act of mercy".'

I believe this criticism reflects a certain confusion and some errors of fact which I should like to clarify. It is certainly true that 'compassion and forbearance' (or if one prefers, 'compassion and forbearance for an offender') is a perfectly legitimate sense of the word 'mercy'. To have mercy in this sense is to feel sorrow and pity for, as well as to overlook the guilt of, a being who deserves punishment. In this sense it is true to say that no treatment of a patient, that is, no treatment of someone who merely suffers can ever be merciful. But this in no way entails that it is a mistake to use the word in any other sense. By distinguishing between being merciful to the guilty and being merciful to those who suffer from disease and illness, one does not make a mistake. To use language differently is not necessarily to use it incorrectly.

The only adequate basis for correctness in a living language has to be the usage of native speakers of that language. Certain sequences of sounds have certain meaning only by virtue of the tacit agreement of the general community of speakers. This community can, under certain conditions, revoke its consent to established rules and set up new ones. Nevertheless, at any given time we can refer to the rules which are in force. We can also refer to violations of these rules.

A misdescription is just one of the possible kinds of violations. A misdescription occurs when a person uses a name to convey characteristics which a fluent English speaker would never associate with that name. It is, therefore, a mistake if someone asks 'What is mercy?' and you point to an act of painting and say, 'That is mercy'. But it is not a mistake to point to an act – an act which offers the kindest possible treatment to someone in great need – and say that 'That is mercy'. It is not a mistake because this is one way, a very common way, in which fluent English speakers use the word.

We now turn to the other objection. Here the critic makes a distinction between intention and fulfilment, between having kind intentions and being kind. He reminds us that wanting to be kind and being kind are two different things. And he maintains that the advocates of euthanasia neglect the more important question of whether or not the actual killing is really kind. He concludes that euthanasia is not merciful because, with all the safeguards, the proposed act of killing is not kind.

Two reasons are usually offered in support of this objection. Each makes a different point. They are :

(1) We are being kind only if we do what some God would do. And to be kind in His way is not to kill but to cure.

(2) The proposed act of killing is not kind because we cannot prove, that is, we cannot provide empirical evidence that it is kind.

As to (1), if matching this God's ability to be kind is the only type of kindness the critic acknowledges, then he confuses kindness with perfection. But kindness is not synonymous with perfection. Every perfect act may be kind but not every kind act is perfect. The critic is demanding that we act as if we were living in a perfect world. Instead of asking, 'What should we do in our present situation?' he asks, 'What would we do if this were a perfect world?' There is only one answer. If this were a perfect world he would not have to ask the question.

I do not wish to be misunderstood. It is one thing to suggest that we emulate some God. It is another to demand that we do what this God himself would do or else do nothing. This last demand is unreasonable. It is unreasonable because we are not gods. It is unreasonable because, within the limits of human endeavour, we can be kind.

As to (2) : I think there is a reason why this criticism cannot be regarded as sufficient, but it seems not unlikely that it is partially correct. It is true that we cannot prove that an act is kind in the same way and to the same extent that we can prove, let us say, that an act is an act of running. But what follows from this? Only that it is usually more difficult to supply evidence for the former than for the latter. It does not follow that we cannot supply evidence to show that a given act is kind.

Suppose we have a case of disseminated carcinoma metastasis before us. That is, a case of cancer where the cancerous cells have spread and have developed fully throughout the body. It is a case that meets all the conditions outlined earlier. We know (i) that the patient has excruciating pain; (ii) that as a result of this condition it is beyond reasonable doubt, a reasonable medical doubt, that the patient has to die; (iii) that the patient, when told of his condition, voluntarily favours some means of 'easy death'; and (iv) that aside from the desire to help the patient no other considerations are relevant. Now it is not easy to know all these things. I am not suggesting that it is. Nor am I saying that such cases are as common as some advocates of euthanasia would have us believe. What I am suggesting is that if there are such cases then, in these cases, it would be kind to kill. It would be kind because all the evidence indicates that this would be the most helpful thing we could do for the patient.

In other words, I am claiming that there is a sense of the word 'mercy' on the basis of which we can correctly say that a merciful act needs to be kind and that a kind act needs to be a helpful one. And that when we examine the evidence in cases like our paradigm case, we know that the proposed act of euthanasia is the kindest possible treatment, because we know that it is the most helpful thing we can do.

7

Kindness

Native speakers of English are equipped with a linguistic sensitivity to the distinction between kind and non-kind acts. This is a way of saying that in speech certain characteristics (or sets of characteristics) are associated with the adjective 'kind'. This information enables us to draw lines, or at least to distinguish roughly between certain acts or actions. I say roughly because the information available does not allow for unanimity when native speakers face certain situations. For example, it is difficult to conceive how the torturing of a six-month-old child can be called kind treatment and still be consistent with normal linguistic intuitions. But there are situations in which these intuitions seem to break down. Some are common occurrences: the problem of whether or not it is kind in a specific situation to help a child do his homework, to tell the truth, to forgive harmful members of a family, and the like. Others are not so common. Having to decide whether or not it is kind to withdraw extraordinary medical support (from, let us say, a child suffering from advanced cerebral arteriosclerosis) is neither a relatively common occurrence nor an easy question.

But even if it be clear in what direction kindness lies, there remains the question of what ought to be done. For even if we could agree that the withdrawal of extraordinary medical support is a kind act, it would not follow that we are always under an obligation to be kind. Evidently, two questions are at issue: What are the characteristics of a kind act? To what extent are we obligated to act kindly?

I

Let us begin by comparing two situations. In the first, we find three men passing a derelict who has just been robbed, stripped and beaten, and left half dead. The first man who passes by feels compassion, but proposes that nothing be done (case 1); the second feels compassion and suggests that the man be taken to the hospital (case 2); the third has no special feelings for the man but believes he ought to be helped, and therefore urges that he be taken to the hospital for medical treatment (case 3). Consider a parallel situation. Here we find three physicians attending a patient who, as a direct result of his condition (disseminated carcinoma metastasis), must shortly die. When told of his condition, the patient voluntarily favours some means of 'easy death'. The first physician feels compassion but suggests that nothing be done aside from normal medical support (case 4); the second feels compassion and urges that the patient be painlessly 'put to sleep', that is, deliberately killed (case 5); the third agrees with the latter proposal, but has no special feeling of sympathy for the patient (case 6).

The question is, which, if any, of the proposed acts are kind?

I suggest that initially we maintain that an act is kind only if it is intended and actually results in helpful treatment. Or, more formally :

> *kind* → (adj.) [act], [human], [intended to be helpful], [resulting in helpful treatment].

Applying these conditions, we obtain the following : Case 1 is not an example of a kind act, since the mere having of a feeling is not an external act. Cases 2 and 3 are examples of kind acts. Case 4 is not, even though it seems to be more problematic than Case 1. A patient who knows he is before death's door may only want those around him to feel compassion, yet it is difficult to understand how the mere existence of a feeling (as opposed to the expression of that feeling) might be construed as a kind act.

Cases 5 and 6 are examples of kindness in spite of the fact that, generally speaking, killing is not a kind act, at least not from the recipient's point of view.

What this comes to, as far as semantics is concerned, is that the notion of kindness is based upon, yet differs from, that of help. Help is the facilitation of a process or state of being. Not to facilitate is not to help. Similarly, one can help someone to do almost anything : lift a box, become happy, or die painlessly. One can help someone to help himself, and, odd as it may seem, one can help someone to harm himself; yet we shrink from saying that helping someone to harm himself is a kind act. Evidently, this reluctance is based upon a distinction between positive and negative help, and the tacit understanding that only positive help is kind.

Help and kindness differ in other interesting respects. An act may be helpful without the actor intending it to be so. For example, one might be helped by finding food that someone has thrown away. Since the help was not intended, however, throwing the food away cannot be considered a kind act. The distinction that I wish to make can best be brought out by the following example. Suppose we have a psychotic psychotherapist who intends not to help his patients, but to harm them. The method is simple. He refuses to make any concession in fees or appointment hours; more important, he refuses to give praise, encouragement, or any advice. Despite these and similar efforts, his patients do amazingly well. Instead of being harmful, the chronic frustration stimulates self-reliance and the development of a healthy independence. How, then, should the therapist's acts of omission be labelled? Surely we must say that the therapy, although not kindly, was helpful.

In contrast to this are acts which, although motivated by the sincere desire to help, have harmful consequences. In one of his fables, Aesop tells of apes who, having given birth to twins, lavish affection on only one of them. In her intense desire to care for the one child, the mother holds him to her breast so tightly that he is smothered to death. Obviously, the road to hell is sometimes paved with good intentions. Not so obvious, I fear, is the recognition that harm intended as help is neither helpful nor kind, and that kindness results only from the combination of good intentions and beneficial consequences.

II

At this point several objections may come to mind. The first is that the foregoing analysis seriously departs from ordinary speech, and that this, in itself, is reprehensible. What, it may be asked, about native speakers who insist that a kind act must be compassionate in nature? Or those who maintain that unwanted kindness is not kindness?

Now it is true that many speakers insist that a kind act must be compassionate in nature, that there must be a feeling of sympathy and a concomitant desire to help to alleviate suffering or need. Hence, compassion becomes (or is) a necessary condition for kindness. Now I am inclined to believe that the requirement of compassion is too strong a condition. Admittedly, an act which is helpful and motivated by compassion is a kind act. But what follows from this? Are these particular feelings necessary? I think not. What is necessary is an intention, namely, the intention to help. Hence, the Samaritan who intends to help, and actually does so, is one who acts kindly. Of course, the Samaritan who has compassion and, because of it, acts to alleviate suffering is also acting kindly. But we make this judgment because we assume (and I think correctly) that one cannot act out of compassion without having certain intentions.

There is another 'ordinary speech objection' that must be considered. Kind acts, we are told, necessarily relate to that form of desire called wanting. An act is kind (in this sense) only if it is in accord with certain dispositions of, or judgments made by, its recipient; or, more simply, unwanted kindness is not really kindness.

Even if we concede that a connection is often (though not always) made between wanting and the *appraisal* of a kind act, this does not alter the fact that to define kindness either partly or wholly in terms of wanting leads to absurdities. Consider the following examples. If, in Case 1, all the derelict wants is compassion, then the act is kind; if, however, compassion is unwanted, the act becomes unkind. If, in Case 3, medical treatment is not wanted (for instance if the person is suicidal and wants to die), then taking him to the hospital is not a kind act. The most bizarre consequence occurs in an altered version of Case 2. Suppose the derelict in question confuses compassion with pity, and hates being pitied. But suppose he also wants medical treatment. The compassion is unwanted, but the medical treatment is wanted. Is the proposed act kind or not? Are we to say that wants are conjunctively related in such a manner that one denial falsifies a complex statement? Are we therefore to say that the act as a whole is not kind? Or is it best to scrap the notion that wanting is a necessary condition?

Surely it is best to scrap the notion, or at least relegate it to its proper position.[1] For one thing, wanting or not wanting does not change the nature of external acts. Just as an unwanted fire is a fire, unwanted kindness is still kindness. Second, it is difficult to understand how wanting could remain only a necessary condition. By its very nature it will usually (and perhaps must) dominate and become the necessary and sufficient condition. This is most objectionable for it leads to a series of further absurdities. All wanted services (having one's ashtrays cleaned, having a repairman mend one's typewriter, and so forth), whether paid for or not, become kind acts, although they would normally be restricted to the class of helpful ones. Moreover, if Tommy Jones wanted to drink an overdose of strychnine, and we gave it to him, the act would be kind.

I should like to examine briefly another objection: that the act of killing cannot follow from the statement that we should act benevolently. Although this is not exactly the claim made in

---

[1] The proper and underlying question is a moral one, namely, whether or not one ought to be kind if such an action conflicts with the wishes, or consenting opinion, of the recipient.

Cases 5 and 6, it is tacitly assumed that killing and kindness are
not logically incompatible.

According to Professor Goodrich this is an error and one of no
small magnitude. He argues that there is something logically odd
in the idea that it may be a kindness to an animal or human
being to end its existence.[2]

> An individual does not exist through the process of dying in
> the same way as he exists through other processes. Dying is
> just ceasing to exist, and one cannot exist through the
> process of ceasing to exist. So how can we say that it is for
> the good of the individual to die?[3]

Or, as stated by Goodrich in the linguistic mode : to say that 'X
would benefit by dying (i.e., by ceasing to exist)' implies that we
can say something like 'X is benefiting by ceasing to exist'. But
to say that 'X is benefiting by ceasing to exist' implies that X
exists through ceasing to exist, which is self-contradictory.

This analysis is mistaken. First, the word 'extermination' or
its cognates may be synonymous with 'ceasing to exist', but dying
is not. Second, there is a difference between stages in a process
and the terminal stage of that process (that is, it is one thing to
be dying and another to be dead). Finally, just as there is nothing
logically odd about saying that we can help a dying patient by
making him more comfortable, there is nothing odd about saying
that we can help a person by hastening the process of dying. That
we are helping, that we are in fact being kind, may or may not
be true, but the claim is not self-contradictory.

An objection related to Goodrich's analysis is the final one I
wish to consider here. It is that the original definition and the
notion used in reply to possible criticism differ, and that the latter
is considerably richer. If this is true, then our definition must be
qualified somewhat (though not abandoned).

When we say that the service or help which is paid for is not

[2] T. Goodrich, 'The Morality of Killing', *Philosophy*, Vol. 44, No. 168
(1969), pp. 127–139.
[3] Ibid., p. 131.

kind, the implication is that to act with the expectation of receiving remuneration or the like is not to act kindly. The point is simple enough. But the question is, what should we add to our definiens, or what are the appropriate semantic markers? To add [. . . and done without expectation of receiving remuneration or the like][4] seems to be an improvement. Yet the phrase 'or the like' is something of a 'hooker', and perhaps should be replaced with something less vague. Additions should also be made in the last marker. For kindness is not only act-specific, it is recipient-specific. Hence, we should change the marker to read: [resulting in helpful treatment for the intended recipient]. This addition may be superfluous, but on this point, I suspect it is better to err on the side of caution, for what is kind for one man may not be kind for his family, other groups, or humanity as a whole.

A needed change, and to my mind the most difficult to make, is to find a more adequate substitute for the phrase 'helpful treatment'. Of course, we can substitute the phrase 'positive help', but this seems to be unnecessarily evasive. The same would be true of such phrases as 'real', 'genuine', or 'authentic help'. Probably the best solution, though it is far from perfect, is to use the term 'beneficial'. Given these changes we can now say that an act is kind only if it is intended to be helpful, is done without the expectation of receiving remuneration (or the like), and results in beneficial treatment for the intended recipient. The graphic representation would be:

kind → (adj.) [act], [human], [intended to be helpful], [done without expectation of receiving remuneration or the like], [resulting in beneficial treatment for the intended recipient].

Such results may seem messy and quite unacceptable to many who demand absolute clarity and pristine simplicity in definitions. But I see no immediate or easy way out when the intent is to

[4] I am grateful to Stephen Nathanson for this particular wording and for other helpful suggestions.

D

map this complex aspect of reality, or at least to explicate ordinary language's attempt to do so. I am aware that a fully adequate mapping requires description of at least benevolent and merciful acts. Nor am I prepared to claim that the notions of help and benefit have (for all the purposes of human inquiry) been made sufficiently clear. All this work is yet to be done. What I would insist upon, however, is that we now have a better understanding of the nature of kindness, and can therefore more intelligently raise the question of obligation.

III

An obligation exists if (perhaps only if) the end in view is (i) not sufficiently impelled by need or natural desire; (ii) consistent with the possibilities of human nature or social systems; and (iii) capable of being universalized because it is a corollary of the principle that basic needs ought to be met and gratuitous suffering avoided. Although plagued by difficulties (the present elusiveness of the terms 'need', 'possibilities of human nature', 'gratuitous suffering' – to name a few), this view is not an unattractive one. Its great merit is that it allows men to know with reasonable assurance which acts are obligatory without being dependent on the actual practice of a social group. We avoid the Scylla of saying that the ontological status of an obligation is the same as that of actual practice or commitment, and the Charybdis of claiming that obligations (like unicorns) are non-existent.

It may be obvious from what has just been said that consent is not necessary for the existence of an obligation. The point is a logical one. The existence of X is one question; the acceptance of X's existence another. For example, there is an obligation to pay one's debts, and most men recognize this. But there is also an obligation in certain situations to tell the whole truth or present all relevant evidence. Yet few (especially those in industry) recognize this, at least not to the extent where it significantly affects their actions. What are we to make of this? We would

scarcely want to say that failure to recognize or accept is synonymous with the non-existence of that obligation. To do so
confuses truth with credibility.

 With regard to the existence of the obligation to be kind, the
situation is essentially as follows. Consider first the question of
whether or not this end in view is impelled by need or natural
desire, to a sufficient degree. We have a certain amount of
evidence that human beings are often disposed to be helpful; in
certain situations human beings come to the assistance of others,
often at the sacrifice of their own interests. On the other hand,
it is generally true that this charitable spirit diminishes as the
circle is extended from that of family and friends to that of
radically different ethnic groups or strangers. What is more, the
increasing amount (perhaps only our increasing awareness) of
child abuse by parents indicates that the kindly family may be
more of a fiction than a fact. In short, the exigencies of human
existence are such as to crush the desire to help others, even those
we purportedly love.

 A question arises at once as to reasonableness. That is, given
what we know about the limitations of human nature and the
hardships of life, we must ask whether or not it is reasonable to
expect human beings to behave in a kindly way. I shall assume
that, although this question can be answered, a definitive answer
is not possible; that, at best, we can succeed only in showing that
one alternative is better – hopefully considerably better – than
others.

 Two radical alternatives to what I am suggesting could be
argued : that it is more reasonable to maintain either that one
should always act with love, or on the contrary, that one should
never help others. The latter runs counter to commonsense and,
to my knowledge, all moral theories. Even the egoist would argue
that helping others is permissible when it does not detract from
one's own interests, and desirable when it directly or indirectly
meets one's own needs.

 In the case of agapeistic love, we are told to extend the greatest
amount of compassion and helpful treatment to the greatest

number of neighbours possible, where 'neighbour' is interpreted to include not only those for whom one has a natural affection, but also strangers and enemies. If this notion did not have such a venerable and honoured tradition, one would be tempted to say that a more impossible ethic is almost unimaginable, and that it ought to be dismissed as beautiful but dangerous rubbish. Indeed, the injunction 'reeks' of impossibility. Consistent empathy for those with whom we have rapport is difficult enough, but to insist that we have this feeling for strongly disliked individuals or groups is not only poor psychology, it is impossible.

A second objection is that the central problem of any moral situation is not usually thought to be that of having certain feelings, but of doing or not doing some specific act or acts. Moreover, to have unlimited feelings, to have unlimited compassion may be possible; but always to extend unlimited help is not. Perhaps the best way to clarify this point is to consider an analogous situation. Suppose a child claims that he is unloved because he has competing siblings and there is not enough love to go around. A parent may truthfully reply that, as a feeling, love cannot be exhausted. Love is not like a quart bottle of milk which runs out after thirty-two ounces have been drunk. Nevertheless, there is a sense in which the child is right. Acts of love are limited. No parent can be in two places at the same time. Moreover, there always seems to be a scarcity of time, a limit to one's energies, and therefore the almost perennial dilemma of deciding who needs help the most.

It seems, then, that love as an ethic is simply not workable. But these comments apply only to those who conceive of love as feeling and exercising the greatest amount of compassion and help. We should remember that other characterizations are possible. And that we would not seriously want to tilt against those who use 'love' honorifically to cover reasonable kindness.

IV

Even if the account given in the preceding section be in the main correct, it seems clear that the unreasonableness of these alternatives does not in itself establish the reasonableness of being kind. There may be other, more reasonable alternatives that have not been examined. In addition, we cannot say that one ought always to be kind, since this formulation is open to objections similar to those made against the love ethic. Without additional constraints, normal men cannot be kind to those they hate or hope to injure. There is also the problem of mutually exclusive choice. When faced with competing vital needs, especially in wartime field conditions, a surgeon can usually only operate on one patient at a time.

Yet it seems niggardly to slip into the principle of benevolence – to say that one ought to help others when to do so conflicts neither with one's own interests nor the exigencies of life. It seems to be giving up too much too soon. Yet, as a principle, benevolence is eminently reasonable. The question is whether we can do better, that is, make a stronger case for the obligation to be kind.

One possibility is that of retrenchment. In spite of the objections made earlier, one could say that we have an absolute duty to be kind, and (I imagine) be content with the knowledge that human beings can meet neither moral expectations nor the problem of conflicting obligations. Another is to back off a little and say not that kindness is absolutely a duty, but rather that each man has a general right to be treated kindly – a right, however, that might be forfeited or suspended under certain circumstances. Another possibility, and the one I wish to opt for, is that each man has a natural right to be treated kindly, and that within this right exist particular obligations. From this point of view, statements of principles of obligation are limited to the form 'one must always do X' (where X stands for an act in which all the relevant circumstances are spelled out). From this point of view, to say that one always ought to be kind is either a mistaken transformation of the right to be treated kindly, or an elliptical way of saying that one ought to be kind in a particular type of situation.

On looking more closely at the natural right to be treated

kindly we see that this doctrine rests on two assumptions : first, that kindness is a secondary need; and second, that since primary or secondary needs exist, they must be met in accordance with the principle that we, as living human beings, ought to avoid unnecessary suffering. There do appear to be valid grounds for making these assumptions; and we actually find the latter to underlie ethical theories which place major value on worldly happiness. We can therefore say that at any rate it is impossible to be genuinely concerned about human happiness and deny the necessity of meeting needs.

Still, the notion that kindness is a secondary need may be something of a puzzle. And, as with most philosophical puzzles, one is content to see if at least some of the important pieces can be filled in. The first of these is to understand that both common-sense and most of social psychology agree that there are biogenic and sociogenic needs.[5] Aside from the more obvious physiochemical needs, a case can be made for the existence of such needs as cognitive understanding, belonging and self-respect. Second, if there are basic human needs and if for reasons of ignorance, scarcity, and so forth, these needs are not being met even minimally, then in addition to the need for X there is a need for help in the recognition and/or procurement of X. Note that this is not to say that kindness is a basic or primary need, but rather that, given these needs and the usual state of affairs, kindness becomes a necessary adjunct.

Generally, we have no doubt that it is right and just to satisfy all basic need claims;[6] indeed, this constitutes the most prominent and easily recognized element of natural rights. There is, then, the understanding that needs shall be met, or approached so as

[5] Two of the best discussions of need-reduction theory are : Marie Jahoda, *Current Concepts of Positive Mental Health* (New York : Basic Books, 1968); and Paul Kurtz, 'Need Reduction and Normal Value', *Journal of Philosophy*, Vol. 55, No. 13 (1958).
[6] Although H. Sidgwick does not, and perhaps would not want to make this particular claim, I am indebted to him for the form of the following argument and the notion that there is some sort of duty to fulfil natural expectations (*Method of Ethics*, 3:4).

to make their fulfilment more easily available, but since even in ordinary times this is inordinately difficult for an individual to accomplish by himself, there is a natural expectation that other members of the groups with which he has primary affiliations (family, church, and so forth) will help him. Although this is, of course, an indefinite and uncertain expectation in a society like ours, where group affiliation and commitments are continually being altered, it is sufficient to nourish the roots of the right to kind treatment. The truth is that all human beings need help at various times in their lives. To be human is to have needs, and to be rational is to expect that where help is necessary it will be given.

To put this differently: it does not make good sense to say that human beings have a right to meet their needs without also saying that they have the right to obtain help in their endeavours when it is needed. What, for example, would it mean to say that an infant had the right to obtain proper nourishment but not the right to be aided in obtaining food? Or that we have the right to health but not the right to obtain adequate health care? Surely the right to satisfy a need without the correlate right to receive help is a hollow mockery.

8

Towards Formulating a Precise Definition of the Word 'Kind'

Bertrand Russell tells the story about a secret society of physiologists who, upon discovering an elixir which would make people kind, refuse to administer it because they are not themselves kind. He concludes that 'only kindliness can save the world, and even if we know how to produce kindliness we should not do so unless we were already kindly'.[1] Putting Russell's paradoxical jibe aside, I think we may fairly conclude that if the only road to human salvation is the way of kindness, it is vital to understand what constitutes kindly behaviour. Or, from a linguistic point of view, the question is, given the sense in which it is used to refer to external human acts, what is meant by the word 'kind'?

The assumption being made here is that kindness is a type of overt help, and therefore that the fundamental question is how to distinguish between acts of kindness and helpfulness.

My sentiment initially was to conceive of helpfulness as 'the facilitation of a process' and kindness as 'an act intended to result and resulting in helpful treatment'. However, it shortly became clear that this characterization was inadequate. For one thing, kindness entails not merely helping, but giving positive help; for example, assisting someone to take an overdose of strychnine may be helpful but is seldom construed as being a kind act. For another, the characterization is so broad that it denotatively admits all helpful acts whether they be paid for or not. Thus we would have to say that the acts of a plumber, electrician,

---

[1] Bertrand Russell, *Icarus or the Future of Science* (New York: E. P. Dutton, 1924), p. 62.

90

or mercenary are necessarily kindly ones which, to my mind, is somewhat bizarre. Finally, since kindness is recipient-specific, we should have to indicate that a kind act is one which 'results in beneficial treatment for the intended recipient'. Given these considerations I thought we might want to say that an act is kind only if it is intended to be helpful, is done without the expectation of receiving remuneration (or the like), and results in beneficial treatment for the intended recipient.

The difficulty with this characterization is that it is over-restrictive. Very few human acts are done without *some* expectation of receiving remuneration or the like. The Boy Scout, for example, who helps an elderly person to cross the street seldom does so out of purely altruistic motives. Similarly, the Good Samaritan may in part be motivated by the desire for eternal rewards or other selfish ends. I do not think we want to rule out their actions as being kindly merely because they are not purely altruistic.

In order to remedy this defect I suggest that we say that an act is kind only if it (a) is intended to be helpful; (b) is done so that, if there be any expectation of receiving remuneration (or the like), the individual would nonetheless act, even if it becomes apparent that there is little chance of his expectation being realized; and (c) results in beneficial treatment for the intended recipient. The graphic representation would be :

> *kind* → (adj.) [act], [human], [intended to be helpful], [done so that, if there be any expectation of receiving remuneration (or the like), the individual would nonetheless act, even if it becomes apparent that there is little chance of his expectation being realized], [resulting in beneficial treatment for the intended recipient].

9

Understanding the Case for Beneficent Euthanasia

When I first became interested in the problem of euthanasia, I was most impressed by the polarization of views and by the fact that few disputants believed that there was middle ground for agreement. Almost all critics of euthanasia consider it to be morally outrageous, while advocates urge the very opposite. According to the critics it is almost self-evident that euthanasia is morally wrong, and therefore unjustifiable homicide. To the advocates it seems to be equally obvious that a moral man is obligated to avoid, and help to reduce, needless misery, and that non-involuntary euthanasia ought therefore to be legalized. The disagreement is further aggravated by vicious name-calling. Opponents allegedly are cruel and heartless, advocates are heinous and barbaric murderers. Given this atmosphere, it is little wonder that underlying issues remain obscure and that disagreement is so rampant.

Understanding depends on, and is proportionate to, the degree to which certain answers are known. In the case of euthanasia the most relevant questions seem to be as follows: Are there powerful underlying sociological forces which explain the deep-rooted resistance? Does the term 'euthanasia', in itself, often generate misunderstanding and needless disagreement? Is it true that all killing produces a brutal and tyrannous state of mind, and that euthanasia must therefore be the first step on a slippery descent into legalized mass murder? Are acts of beneficent euthanasia unjust? Finally, what is kindness or beneficence, and to what extent are we obligated to act kindly?

The primary purpose of this essay is to explore these questions and locate the true sources of disagreement. The second objective is more ambitious. I am inclined to believe, and hope to show, that a much better case can be made for euthanasia than against it, and that in certain situations the moral man is obligated to kill.

It would be unrealistic to suggest that within the brief compass of this chapter we can do more than touch upon problems of theological belief and language, and the arguments from justice and kindness. Yet the problems and arguments exist. And philosophers should begin to worry more seriously about ethical theories which refuse to, or cannot, adequately face up to the question of whether killing is ever justified, and if so under what circumstances. For Camus was right in crying out that 'we shall be capable of nothing until we know whether we have the right to kill our fellow-men, or the right to let them be killed'.[1]

I

Before explicating what is meant by 'beneficent euthanasia', I wish to say a few words about the role of theology. Since theology and ethics are logically independent,[2] there is no need within the context of moral argument to reply to theological objections. I will, however, venture to suggest that our *attitude* toward euthanasia in general – perhaps more so than toward any other moral issue – is profoundly effected by the existence of theological ideas, whether these ideas are openly accepted or not. The first of these ideas is the belief that only God has absolute dominion over human life. The second is that death is a punishment, and – except for extreme torture – the worst form. The third, and perhaps most interesting, is the belief that deliberately to kill an

[1] Albert Camus, *The Rebel* (London: Penguin Books, 1969; New York: Alfred A. Knopf, 1954), p. 12.

[2] For supporting arguments, see: A. J. Ayer, in *Religion and the Intellectuals: A Symposium* (New York: Partisan Review, 1950), pp. 31–2; Kai Nielsen, 'Some Remarks on the Independence of Morality from Religion', *Mind*, No. 70, April, 1961, pp. 175–186, and 'God and the Good: Does Morality Need Religion?', *Theology Today*, Vol. 21, No. 1 (1964), pp. 47–58.

innocent human being is to place one's own immortal soul in the gravest jeopardy.

Lest what I am saying be misunderstood, I am not suggesting that these beliefs be rejected merely because they are theological. What I am suggesting is (1) that since theological belief alone cannot entail moral conclusions, there is need for independent moral discernment; (2) that religious tenets play a profoundly important, though not necessarily a noticeable, sociological role in the case of euthanasia; and (3) that although philosophers are often quick to distinguish between theological aversion and moral condemnation, there is no easy way to distinguish between prejudices or valueless instincts and real judgments of value, especially when the former have been given great weight by tradition and the cumulative force of authority.

Let us now turn to the question of what is meant by the word 'euthanasia'. Etymologically, it means *eu*, good + *thanasia,* death. I would conjecture that, given its original use, 'death' meant 'induced death', and 'good' meant 'good for its recipient'. But over years of use, the meaning of the term has so loosened that it is now correctly used to refer to almost any death or means of death, which from one or more perspectives may be viewed as being of a good or better kind. In this sense a loving parent who painlessly kills a hopelessly comatose child, a nurse who upon request administers an overdose of narcotics to a terminally ill patient, or a Nazi physician who injects a fatal dose of phenol to a non-consenting prisoner are all practising euthanasia.

What is needed is not a change in definition, nor reductionism,[3] but a more adequate characterization of the broad sense of this term. I suggest that we provide one which, while preserving the scope for contemporary usage, more clearly explicates the notion of a 'good' death, and does so without begging important moral

---

[3] It would hardly be of value to suggest that we return to the 'tighter' meaning of the original term. Reductionism may have its logical merits, but it is not linguistically feasible. For it is almost impossible to erase, or completely substitute for, conventions currently in wide use. Therefore, what I propose to do is to retain the broader meaning, and add qualifiers when necessary.

questions. It seems clear, for example, that the word should not
be defined as 'mercy murder' or its like, since this by definition
entails that the act must be unethical. By the same token it should
not be defined as 'the act or practice of morally ending the life
of an incurable sufferer', since this also begs the moral question.
What, then, can be done? We may, I suggest, define 'euthanasia'
as 'the painless inducement of a quick death'. This characterization adds a needed element of clarity, preserves the modern
paradigmatic use of the term, and leaves open the possibility of
distinguishing moral and immoral acts of euthanasia.

Since I am urging that there is a prima facie obligation to
consent to acting kindly, the next question is, what is meant by
kind or beneficent euthanasia? There are various senses of the
word 'kind'. One of the most important is the sense in which
we say that an act is kind if it (a) is intended to be helpful; (b)
is done so that, if there be any expectation of receiving remuneration (or the like), the individual would nonetheless act even if it
became apparent that there was little chance of his expectation
being realized; and (c) results in beneficial treatment for the
intended recipient.[4] The Boy or Girl Scout helping an elderly
man or woman cross the street, or the proverbial Good Samaritan,
are paradigm cases of kindness.

This means that the necessary, and perhaps sufficient, conditions for beneficent euthanasia are that the act must involve a
painless inducement of a quick death; that the act must result
in beneficial treatment for the intended recipient; and that, aside
from the desire to help the recipient, no other considerations are
relevant (a combination of conditions (a) and (b)). There are
also paradigms of beneficent euthanasia. On the surface they
seem unusually complex. The first occurs when we know (i) that
the patient is suffering from an irremediable condition such as
disseminated carcinoma metastasis; (ii) that the patient has
excruciating pain; (iii) that as a result of his condition it is beyond
a reasonable medical doubt that the patient has to die; (iv) that

---

[4] For discussion of alternative views and the difficulties of an earlier
formulation, see pp. 78–84, 90–91.

the patient when told of his condition voluntarily favours some means of 'easy death'; and (v) that aside from the desire to help the patient no other conditions are relevant. By contrast, the second case is much more revealing. This occurs when we know (i) that a child is born without limbs, sight, hearing, or a functioning cerebral cortex; (ii) although unable to move a muscle, he suffers no pain; (iii) that as long as he is fed and otherwise cared for, death is not imminent; and (iv) that aside from the desire to help the patient, no other conditions are relevant. The striking thing about these situations is the extent to which they differ. Putting aside their common features (something being seriously and irremediably wrong, and the motivation being essentially the wish to help), the only other 'feature' they share is that the induced death probably would be viewed by most men as an act of kindness.[5] The importance of this observation can hardly be overestimated, for if true it means that considerations of free choice, the imminence of death, and/or the existence of pain are not always relevant, at least not to judgments of kindness.

II

The initial argument on behalf of beneficent euthanasia is that, since it is kind treatment, and since society and its members each have a prima facie (though not equal) obligation to treat members kindly, it follows that beneficent euthanasia is a prima facie obligation. This seems straightforward, and so obviously correct that most advocates would be content to let the matter end here. Critics, however, believe the argument to be irrelevant and/or fallacious.

By far the most popular objection is the 'wedge' or 'slippery slope' argument, which tells us that 'once the principle of the sanctity of human life is abandoned, or the propaganda accepted that to uphold it is old-fashioned, prejudiced or superstitious, the

---

[5] Let us not pursue the question of whether the case of the brain-damaged child is as non-controversial as that of the carcinoma case; obviously it is not. The more interesting point is this. The inability of such a child to be aware of his condition does not mean that he cannot be treated kindly.

way is open to the raising of – and the satisfaction of – a demand for so-called euthanasia for the severely crippled, the aged, and ultimately for all who are a burden on community services and the public purse.'[6] Again, one of the most effectively formulated arguments in the literature is that :

 It is true that the 'wedge' objection can always be advanced, the horrors can always be paraded. But it is less true that on some occasions the objection is much more valid than it is on others. One reason why the 'parade of horrors' cannot be too lightly discussed in the particular instance is that Miss Voluntary Euthanasia is not likely to be going it alone for very long. Many of her admirers . . . would be neither surprised nor distressed to see her joined by Miss Euthanatize the Congenital Idiot and Miss Euthanatize the Permanently Insane and Miss Euthanatize the Senile Dementia. And these lasses – whether or not they themselves constitute a 'parade of horrors' – certainly make excellent majorettes for such a parade. . . .

 Another reason why the 'parade of horrors' argument cannot be dismissed in this particular instance, it seems to me, is that the parade *has* taken place in our time and the order of procession has been headed by killing the 'incurables' and the 'useless'. . . . The apparent innocuousness of Germany's 'small beginnings' is perhaps best shown by the fact that German Jews were at first excluded from the programme. For it was originally conceived that 'the blessing of euthanasia should be granted only to [true] Germans'.[7]

The merit of this argument is that Kamisar is not merely saying that a slide *can* occur, but is suggesting rather strongly that it *must* occur. The question is, why the necessity?

The first explanation, which is suggested by the use of sexual metaphors, is that there is something terribly seductive about the

[6] Jonathan Gould *et al.*, 'The Ethics of Euthanasia', in *Your Death Warrant? The Implications of Euthanasia*, edited by Jonathan Gould and Lord Craigmyle (London: Geoffrey Chapman, 1971), p. 88.
[7] Yale Kamisar, 'Euthanasia Legislation: Some Non-Religious Objections', in *Euthanasia and the Right to Death*, op. cit., pp. 115–116.

nature of killing, especially when it is given legal sanction. The second, and Kamisar's analysis withstanding, is that the practice of euthanasia was not the result of a slide, but was rather the direct consequence of the Nazis' political ideology – an ideology which rested upon the principle that if proper political authorities believed killing could serve the greater good of a true Germany, then those in question not only were expendable but ought to have been sacrificed for the greater good.

Of the two explanations, the first may be ruled out. There is simply no evidence that killing *per se* is contagious, and overwhelming evidence to show that it is not. It is true that people who believe that it is right to kill Gypsies, Jews, or anyone else, provided their death may profit the State, will probably continue to kill if they continue to have the power to do so. But this is not evidence of the seductiveness of killing. Rather it is evidence that when men have almost unlimited power, their actions will be consistent with their beliefs, and when their beliefs entail needless cruelty, so will their actions.

Attractive as this view is, I cannot resist the feeling that Kamisar's argument, and most of the analogies with the Nazi experience, gain an air of plausibility from other sources.

Let us begin with the question of killing. I certainly have suggested, and do maintain, that if one has to kill, then euthanasia (the painless inducement of a quick death) is the kindest way. This is based upon the commonsense understanding that if death must come, it had best be swift and painless. But this is *not* to say that to use the kindest way of killing is synonymous with being kind. The act of putting 'incurables' and the 'useless' painlessly and quickly 'to sleep', for the sole purpose of being relieved of the burden of providing adequate care, may be the kindest way of killing, but is by no stretch of the imagination a kind act. Similarly, injecting phenol into the veins of prisoners for purposes of economic and speedy killing is obviously not a kind act. No doubt there are cases where the line between a kind aspect and the act as a whole is difficult to draw. It may also be conceded that in those special cases, as when concentration camp prisoners were undergoing the brutal tortures of so-called medical experimentation, their being killed was, indeed, often a blessing. But even if all this be admitted, great care should be taken not to confuse using the kindest way of killing with being kind – and, more important, not to believe mistakenly that the Nazi practitioners of euthanasia were acting kindly when indeed most of their actions were paradigms of cruelty.

What worries me most about these 'wedge' arguments is they seem to be based upon the assumption, first, that all theories of euthanasia ultimately rest upon a principle of utility, and second, that all theories of utility are the same as those held by the Nazis. This latter assumption is comparatively simple, and might no doubt be laid to rest by pointing to the diversity of utilitarian positions. But it is not this problem that I wish to discuss. What I wish to consider is why so many opponents of euthanasia believe the basic theory behind euthanasia is the same as that held by the Nazis.

Euthanasia has been advocated by most of its champions chiefly as a means of reducing human misery, and more particularly as a way of maximizing kind or loving treatment. To these men and women, it has seemed, accordingly, to have little to do with fiscal matters or economic consequences. Some of its advocates, however, have written as if the question of fiscal utility were of prime importance. They argue that there is a need to save the young from the great cost of caring for those who are irremediably ill and to save the general public from staggering and unnecessary medical expense, adding that euthanasia legislation 'might save the country a few billion dollars a year'. I do not know whether such writers would want to say that this is the sole justification, or whether it has merely become fashionable to reduce all ethical problems to a matter of economics but, for whatever reasons, this approach generates fear and, to a degree, warrants the parade of Nazi horrors.

It is vital, but not enough, to distinguish between principles of utility and beneficence or to say that for most advocates the primary goal is that of reducing misery and maximizing kind or loving treatment. We must admit, however reluctantly, that there are less desirable and immoral forms of euthanasia. More important, all men ought to stand firm in opposition to such practices. For of all forms of moral hypocrisy, the most repugnant is to act cruelly under the guise of kindness. This is the first thing that should be done.

The second is to distinguish between the kindest way of doing X and the kindest way of treating a human being as a human being. For the objective is not merely death with dignity, but that of living and dying with dignity. In this respect critics are quite right. The long-range objective, the goal, is not merely the kind treatment of the injured or the sick, but the kind treatment of all members of society in all their endeavours. The moral rule (which we dub the principle of beneficence) is that in each problematic situation, society owes to each man the maximum amount of help that is consistent with the principles of justice and the realities of human existence.

This means that if there is a 'slide', the result will be that of minimizing suffering and maximizing kindly treatment. Or, to put it otherwise : essentially, we are being told that we must not try to make society into a kinder place because our generation has experienced the Nazi horror. Although the Nazis were neither kind nor merciful, kindness must slip into cruelty, merciful killing must somehow slide into ethnic and political savagery. Why not take the opposite tack? Why not say that, because we view the Nazi experience with such dread, we will make sure Miss Euthanatize the Useless will never again parade? Why not say that, because the thought of Nazi atrocities fills us with moral loathing, we will never again retreat into cruelty – that, rather than be indifferent, we shall establish safeguards and encourage men to act and only act out of kindness and justice?

III

At this juncture the question of justice might most profitably be raised; for some may consent to most of what has been said, yet deny that beneficent euthanasia is just and therefore moral.

One of the most interesting objections is based upon what I should like to call the Libertarian-Property (hereafter referred to as L-P) view of justice. According to this view, a human being possesses a right to those things that properly belong to him by nature, by birth, by gift, or by contract, and we can take morally only what each freely chooses to give. Or, stated as a substantive principle: 'From each according to his choice to each according to what properly belongs to him.' The major allegation is that whatever its source, human life is the property neither of the individual nor of the state, and therefore all homicide is intrinsically unjust.

This, I believe, explains why there is not only opposition to involuntary but also to voluntary euthanasia. At first sight to say 'each according to choice' seems to suggest that a man does not treat another unjustly when he accedes to that individual's considered request. But then quickly to add, 'to each according to what properly belongs to him', with a further proviso that 'a human being's life does not properly belong to him', certainly closes the door on voluntary euthanasia. For the combination entails that it is never perfectly just to take either one's own or the life of another human being.

The L-P proposal consists of two parts: (i) that goods or services should be supplied on the basis of natural or acquired property; (ii) that all responsible human beings should be free to choose what they want to contribute. These two proposals are not necessarily inseparable, nor does either entail the rejection of euthanasia *per se*, although both are generally so interpreted. As regards the first, and leaving aside the exciting question of whether this is an adequate principle of distributive justice,[8] the conclusions drawn are at best dubious.

Let us admit that we can, and perhaps in some situations should, conceive of life as something which belongs to an indivi-

---

[8] Suffice it to say here that, unless all members of a community have equal chance and opportunity to acquire property, the proposal comes down to nothing more than a clandestine form of inegalitarianism.

dual by nature. This metaphorical use of 'belong' has drawbacks, but I suspect that no serious harm follows from it. The question is, if a human being's life belongs to him, then what are the grounds for saying that it does not *properly* belong to him?

It is sheer nonsense to pretend that vestigial religious tenets are not at work here. According to *Deuteronomy* (32 : 39), God will kill and God will make to live. Many religious believers therefore conclude that it belongs to God alone to pronounce the sentence of life or death. Paradoxically, many men who do not believe in God nevertheless believe that all human life properly belongs to Him. But if this be the purported justification, then it clearly rests on more than a property view of justice. As such it falls easy prey to our objections to a purely theological ethic.

It would, however, be an undue simplification to suppose that a theory of divine ownership is the sole source of this belief. There is a non-theological variant of what is really much the same doctrine. It consists in saying that, since every man is part of the community, both his body and his life belongs to that community. Here the authority is no longer God's Will, but Community Will. The danger, of course, is that Community Will is often interpreted as being synonymous with God's Will, and then the argument slips back and suffers from the same defects as the theological one.

But such a slip is not necessary. The claim would be that behind Community Will is the authority of general consent – that the rights to life and death are not only freely, but permanently transferred to the community. Admittedly, we now have a more interesting argument; but it is difficult to see how it can be squared with the L-P point of view. First, it is clear that man is not 'part' of a community in the sense that his body and life are 'part' of his person. Second (according to a property view of distributive justice), if one naturally possesses and owns anything, it is surely one's body and life. Third, even if one introduces the notion of social contract or of tacit consent, the L-P advocate would be opposed to the idea of completely transferring basic rights, especially the right to life and death; and finally, he would insist (and I think correctly) that the permanent transfer of these rights is a blatant and outrageous denial of the principles of liberty.

As regards the second proposal, it has the advantage of allowing human beings to maintain their sense of dignity through the general exercising of free choice. Other things being equal, this seems to mean that if a responsible individual chooses (or chooses not) to give up his life, then he ought to be free to do so. This part of the proposal also suggests that a person is free to choose only if he is physically and mentally able to choose. This can be interpreted to mean that when a person is not free in this sense (as, for example, in the case of the comatose child) society may appoint a responsible individual, or when necessary, the state, to act in his behalf. If so, this indicates that voluntary and some forms of non-voluntary (not involuntary) euthanasia are consistent with the Libertarian aspect of the proposal.

The fundamental value of liberty is that it diminishes the risk of injustice and gives men the sense of dignity they need. It is not always easy to know when a person is not free to choose, nor should the transfer of this obligation be taken lightly. However, when fanatical insistence on consent only brings with it continued or increased misery, and when it is clear that neither justice nor dignity is being served, then we must choose and act on behalf of the interests of the individual. It may be concluded, therefore, that this part of the L-P proposal is consistent with the principle of beneficence, and that all men concerned about human welfare ought to subscribe to it.

There are other objections which are commonly raised against euthanasia.[9] One of these, and probably the most formidable, is that beneficent euthanasia is the killing of an innocent human being, and as such is unjust. Unlike the abortion controversy, both parties to this dispute agree there is no problem concerning the question of innocence. Almost all the intended patients or

[9] The most thorough and convincing presentation of the Catholic case against euthanasia is that by Joseph V. Sullivan, *The Morality of Mercy Killing* (Maryland: The Newman Press, 1950), esp. pp. 26–62. For a listing of additional objections as well as some excellent rebuttals, see: Joseph Fletcher, *Morals and Medicine* (Boston: Beacon Press, 1954), pp. 190–207.

recipients are viewed as being innocent and, it is doubtless important to add, innocent in all the morally significant senses of that term. There is another cardinal area of agreement. At least on the surface, both advocates and opponents agree that, generally speaking, one ought not to kill innocent human beings. Disagreement immediately arises, however, when opponents add that the killing of the innocent is *always* unjust.

An analysis of what underlies this disagreement is difficult, and requires considerable tact. The most difficult aspect is that of the differing attitudes towards death. Most children as they grow up discover that plants and animals die. Some are told that death is a state or an event whereby an organism is permanently released from the constraints of metabolic functioning – or, more simply, that death is a sleep from which plants and animals do not wake. But most are told, or presumably hear, that death occurs when life is taken away. To make matters worse, such children (especially if they receive certain kinds of orthodox religious education), are likely to believe that death is essentially a punishment. And all this is usually reinforced by the child's growing up in an atmosphere where the ideas of blood revenge and retaliatory killing are prevalent.

It is true that a child often witnesses, or knows about, the merciful killing of an animal. Moreover, the killing of the animal is not construed as a form of punishment. But apparently such experiences make little or no impact.

Someone may say that this is interesting by way of explanation, but it is not much of an argument. This is correct, but only to a limited extent. For what I have been urging is that the generalization, 'it is always unjust to kill the innocent', is hastily drawn, and that the major reason for this overstatement is the widespread belief that killing is always a punishment for its recipient. Or, to cast down a more formidable gauntlet, the opponent of euthanasia has to be able to show why beneficent euthanasia is not a legitimate exception to his law-like injunction.

As regards a more positive argument, the most decisive is based upon a need-reduction theory of value. It recognizes that justice requires that we treat every case which is essentially similar to X in manner Y. Or, negatively stated, 'An act of distributing is at least prima facie unjust if it involves treating differently, or discriminating between, individuals whose cases are similar in all important respects'.[10] Thus if we have the right to a 'good' death, then we have as much right to such treatment as anyone else in essentially similar circumstances. This formal principle, however, does not take us very far, since it fails to specify what basic things are to be distributed. Probably no substantive principle can solve all such problems. Nonetheless, it is important to have one which both represents the 'right to die with dignity' wing of the euthanasia movement, and best approximates the egalitarian idea. The principle reads : 'to each according to basic human needs.'[11] This means that the just society makes the same proportionate contribution to the welfare of each, in an effort to make all as nearly equally well off as possible.[12]

Applying these general considerations to the case at hand, we find that it is necessary, or at any rate more consonant with general intent, to add certain factual claims. One is that all human beings have the basic need for dignity or self-respect. The other is that where killing is restricted to cases of non-involuntary beneficent euthanasia, it is not a punishment, but a matter of meeting a basic need. Let us consider the two paradigm cases. In spite of all that has been said, one could say that these killings are punishments. But this is like observing two black swans, and then insisting that they must be white because one has been taught to believe that this must be true. This is not to suggest that one cannot have punishment with dignity. It is, however, to maintain that in situations like the paradigm cases, there is

---

[10] William K. Frankena, *Some Beliefs About Justice* (University of Kansas: The Lindley Lecture, 1966), p. 4.

[11] The question of what the just society requires of its members is much more difficult. Suffice it here to say that the beliefs of advocates of beneficent euthanasia range from that of the libertarian (From each according to choice to each according to his wants), to that of the traditional socialist (From each according to his ability to each according to his need).

[12] I am indebted to Frankena, op. cit., p. 14, for this formulation.

evidence neither of intent to punish nor actual punishment, and considerable evidence of treatment with kindness and dignity.

It is time to draw together the various aspects of the case for beneficent euthanasia. An act is an act of beneficent euthanasia if, and perhaps only if, it (i) results in the painless inducement of a quick death; (ii) results (i.e., the act as a whole) in beneficial treatment for the intended recipient; (iii) is intended to be helpful; and (iv) is done so that, if there is any expectation of receiving remuneration (or the like), the individual would still act in that manner, even if it becomes apparent that there is little or no chance of his expectation being realized.

This characterization and the principle of beneficence provide the conceptual and moral foundations for the major argument. The argument is that beneficent euthanasia is kind treatment, and since society has a prima facie obligation to treat its members kindly, it follows that beneficent euthanasia is a prima facie obligation. Of the two other important considerations, the first is that proponents of this theory are not advocating, and are strongly opposed to, any theory that solely or ultimately rests upon a principle of economic utility; the second, that if there be any danger of a slide, it is the 'danger' of encouraging men to act kindly.

In addition to the argument from kindness, there is an argument from justice. It has two prongs. The first is that, where an individual is not constrained but physically and mentally is free to choose, his consent is necessary. This is an essential safeguard, for we know that one of the best defences against injustice is that of informed consent. The second is that justice further requires that where possible we are to give to each according to basic needs, and since human beings have a basic need to live and die with dignity, it is just that we treat them accordingly.

IV

I come now to the most exciting, and if valid, most telling objection. Here we are told that the argument from kindness is fallacious. According to this view, euthanasia is not merely kind treatment but the kindest, and therefore there is no moral obligation to extend the kindest possible treatment. While we may be obligated to help a patient – to provide adequate medical care, to make him physically and psychologically comfortable, and so forth – we are in no way obligated to kill.

I do not think it can be questioned that this sentiment is widely held. Many who are made uncomfortable by the plight or suffering of others would, nonetheless, deny that there is an obligation to do all that can be done to help, especially if the help entails killing. It is not altogether easy to decide what is the root cause of this sentiment. But I suspect that interwoven with a general aversion to killing are two closely related but independent claims. The first is that we are simply mistaken as to what is the proper moral injunction. The correct statement is not that society ought to act kindly, but that it ought not to act cruelly. The second is that the principle of beneficence is unrealistic, since it blithely ignores the problem of the scarcity of goods and services, thereby expecting too much from both the individual and society. Let us consider first the question of cruelty.

Both sides to the dispute agree that cruelty ought to be avoided. But they disagree over (i) what constitutes cruelty and (ii) whether or not avoidance of cruelty is morally sufficient. As to (i): In a narrow sense of the term, an act is cruel if it deliberately causes unnecessary pain or harm. In its broadest sense, an act or event is cruel if it deliberately causes or allows needless pain or harm. For reasons too complex to enter into here, opponents of euthanasia tend to employ the narrow sense. They recognize the misery of patients such as those represented by our paradigm cases, but would view neither the inflictions nor the reluctance to permanently relieve the sufferers of their plight as acts of cruelty. As a consequence of this position, they are more prone to tolerate and excuse human misery. As to (ii) the trouble with the injunction is that it expresses a taboo morality. It tells us what not to do, but not what to do. Admittedly, a society that avoids cruelty is better than one that does not. But men who accept and so limit their benevolent actions must essentially close their eyes to natural disaster, disease and accident. Unlike the Good Samaritan, they walk past the injured or the sick with a clear conscience. While they do not deliberately harm, they do not necessarily help. I do not doubt that such a society is possible, but what is difficult to understand is why one would associate it with the good life.

Let us take an illustration somewhat removed from the problem of euthanasia : the question of child abuse. The rate of reported incidents of physical abuse for the United States was 8·4 per 100,000 children for 1967 and 9·3 for 1968.[13] These figures say nothing about psychological damage, or of how neglect effects the mortality and morbidity rate of children. Now the man who only opposes cruelty condemns the ill-treatment and victimization of children, but he does not favour long-term preventative help. For example, he is not disposed towards reducing poverty, even though its elimination is likely to reduce this sort of phenomena. Nor is he disposed towards programmes like Head Start, even though the non-violent manner of socialization which is an essential feature of such programmes has a positive and strong effect upon child-rearing attitudes and practices. In short, he is not inclined to do what needs to be done in order to *prevent* such abuse. Yet, I do not wish to give the impression that a principle of beneficence would be sufficient. What I am advocating is that it is a necessary condition, that there must be the desire or felt obligation to extend both short and long-term help.

We now turn to the claim that the principle of beneficence is unrealistic. Here we are told that, although there is a principle of kindness at work, the goods and services available for distribution are of a limited nature, and therefore that a normal society or individual cannot be kind without limit. Moreover, since there is a scarcity, and since society expects its members to have a primary obligation to care for the things they procreate or own,

[13] David G. Gil, *Violence Against Children* (Cambridge, Mass.: Harvard University Press, 1970; London, 1971), pp. 98–99.

the primary obligation is to take care of one's own children and property.

This argument certainly has a good deal of plausibility. It is true to say that, given what most human beings *want*, the supply is both limited and insufficient. But it is not true, given an affluent society like our own, that the supply of what human beings *need* is insufficient, though it is limited, as undoubtedly most things are. Moreover, when we turn to the problem of dying well, the scarcity argument breaks down. For kind killing neither exhausts nor threatens to exhaust our resources. Indeed, if a society is too niggardly to allow its members to live with dignity, then allowing or helping them die with dignity should strike even the most economically-minded of individuals as being a great bargain.

The question as to the degree of kindness morality in general requires is so much more difficult that I shall be content to offer a few more clues.

One may lay it down broadly that no man is morally required *always* to act in the kindest possible manner. Only saints can maintain themselves in this exceptional position, and I do not think we want a moral theory suitable only for saints. Yet it does not seem right to say that one ought *never* to act in the kindest manner, for there are times when we ought to do so even though it is at great sacrifice or effort. In so far as we are convinced of the rightness of this, we are loath to settle for mere benevolence.

The principle of beneficence states that in each problematic situation, society owes to each man the maximum of help that is consistent with the principles of justice and the realities of human existence. This formulation leaves much to be desired. Yet it has the merit of shifting from the notion of individual to that of collective responsibility. It recognizes that moral problems arise in situations out of an awareness that something is the matter. It admits that moral solutions are limited by powerful empirical constraints. It enjoins us to consider the kindly treatment of one individual as equally important as the kindly treatment of any other, and that our kindness ought to be distributed so as to make the same proportionate contribution to the welfare of each, in an effort to make all as nearly equally well off as possible. Most important, it reminds us that all human beings at one time or another need – and are entitled to – the assistance of others, and where it is both necessary and reasonable to help, it is our obligation to do so.

Selected Bibliography

Aquinas, St Thomas, 'Of Murder', *Summa Theologica*, 2.2.64, London : Burns Oates & Washbourne, 1929.

Brody, Baruch, 'Thomson on Abortion', *Philosophy and Public Affairs*, Vol. 1, No. 3, 1973.

——, 'Abortion and the Law', *Journal of Philosophy*, Vol. 68, No. 12, 1971.

Callahan, Daniel, 'The Sanctity of Life', in Cutler, Donald R. (ed.), *Updating Life and Death*, Boston : Beacon Press, 1969.

Camus, Albert, 'The Just Assassins', in *Caligula and Three Other Plays*, London : Hamish Hamilton, 1947; New York : Vintage Books, 1958.

——, 'Reflections on the Guillotine', in *Resistance, Rebellion, and Death*, New York : Modern Library, 1963; London : Hamish Hamilton, 1964.

Downing, A. B. (ed.), *Euthanasia and the Right to Death*, London : Peter Owen, 1969; New York : Humanities Press, 1970.

Fletcher, Joseph, 'Euthanasia', in *Morals and Medicine*, Boston : Beacon Press, 1954.

——, 'Elective Death', in Torrey, E. Fuller (ed.), *Ethical Issues in Medicine*, Boston : Little, Brown & Co., 1968.

Freud, Sigmund, 'Thoughts for the Times on War and Death', 1915, in *Collected Papers*, Vol. IV, London : Hogarth Press, 1925.

——, 'Why War?', 1932, in Strachey, James (ed.), *Collected Papers*, Vol. V, London : Hogarth Press, 1951.

Gerber, R. J., 'Abortion : Parameters for Decision', *Ethics*, Vol. 82, No. 2, 1972.

Goodrich, T., 'The Morality of Killing', *Philosophy*, Vol. 44, No. 168, 1969.

Gould, Jonathan and Craigmyle, Lord (eds.), *Your Death Warrant? The Implications of Euthanasia*, London: Geoffrey Chapman, 1971.

Hoffman, Robert, 'The Moral Right to Abortion', *Michigan Quarterly Review*, Vol. 8, No. 4, 1969.

Hook, Sidney, 'The Ethics of Suicide', *International Journal of Ethics*, No. 37, 1927.

Kohl, Marvin, 'The Word "Mercy" and the Problem of Euthanasia', *The American Rationalist*, Vol. 9, No. 10, 1965.

——, 'Abortion and the Argument from Innocence', *Inquiry*, Vol. 14, No. 1 & 2, 1971.

——, 'The Sanctity of Life Principle', in Visscher, Maurice (ed.), *Humanistic Perspectives in Medical Ethics*, New York: Prometheus Books, 1972.

——, 'Abortion and the Slippery Slope', *Dissent*, Fall, 1972.

Lorenz, Konrad, *On Aggression*, Toronto: Bantam Books, 1963; London: Methuen, 1966.

McFadden, Charles, 'Direct Abortion', in *Medical Ethics*, Philadelphia: F. A. Davis & Co., 6th ed., 1967.

Russell, Bertrand, *Justice in War Time*, Chicago: Open Court, 1917.

Schweitzer, Albert, *The Teaching of Reverence for Life*, New York: Holt, Rinehart & Winston, 1965; London: Peter Owen, 1966.

Shils, Edward, 'The Sanctity of Life', in Shils, E., *et al.* (eds), *Life or Death: Ethics and Options*, Seattle: University of Washington Press, 1968.

Sullivan, Joseph V., *The Morality of Mercy Killing*, Maryland: Newman Press, 1950.

Thomson, Judith, 'A Defence of Abortion', *Philosophy and Public Affairs*, Vol. 1, No. 1, 1971.

Wasserstrom, Richard A. (ed.), *War and Morality*, Belmont, California and London: Wadsworth, 1970.

Wertheimer, Roger, 'Understanding the Abortion Argument', *Philosophy and Public Affairs*, Vol. 1, No. 1, 1971.